the end of the alphabet

alphabet

how gen Z can save america

isabel brown

foreword by dave rubin

CENTER
STREET

NASHVILLE   NEW YORK

Center Street
Hachette Book Group
1290 Avenue of the Americas, New York, NY 10104
centerstreet.com
twitter.com/centerstreet

First edition: March 2024

Center Street is a division of Hachette Book Group, Inc. The Center Street name and logo are trademarks of Hachette Book Group, Inc.
The publisher is not responsible for websites (or their content) that are not owned by the publisher.

Center Street books may be purchased in bulk for business, educational, or promotional use. For information, please contact your local bookseller or the Hachette Book Group Special Markets Department at special.markets@hbgusa.com.

Library of Congress Cataloging-in-Publication Data

Names: Brown, Isabel (Podcaster), author. | Rubin, Dave, 1976– writer of foreword.
Title: The end of the alphabet : how Gen Z can save America / Isabel Brown.
Description: Nashville : Center Street, 2024. | Includes bibliographical references.
Identifiers: LCCN 2023040985 | ISBN 9781546006251 (hardcover) | ISBN 9781546006275 (ebook)
Subjects: LCSH: Conservatism—United States. | Generation Z—Political activity—United States. | United States—Politics and government—2021-
Classification: LCC JC573.2.U6 B776 2024 | DDC 320.520973—dc23/eng/20231018
LC record available at https://lccn.loc.gov/2023040985

ISBNs: 9781546006251 (hardcover), 9781546006275 (ebook)

Printed in the United States of America

LSC-C

Printing 1, 2023

To young, punk rock patriots
in every chapter of history:
may our fight never cease to
bring hope to the future.

contents

FOREWORD

Before I tell you a bit about Isabel, and why I'm honored to write the foreword for this book, I'd like to take you on a journey all the way back to the fall of 2015. So get in your DeLorean, make sure the flux capacitor has enough power and join me for the ride...

Twenty-fifteen may not seem too long ago in actual years, but in terms of the temperature of the country it feels like centuries ago. It was a time before the Trump presidency, before COVID, before Black Lives Matter, and even before TikTok. While our political wars had long been raging, our culture wars were just beginning to simmer.

In the fall of that year, I relaunched the Rubin Report after several years of being on the lefty YouTube Young Turks Network. I was on the verge of my own personal political evolution and the world was on the verge of a total media revolution.

One of my first moves with the relaunched Rubin Report was to buck the trend of creating shorter and shorter videos. While this was before TikTok, it was during the explosion of SnapChat and the height of the now defunct six-second-video madness of Vine. Everything was getting shorter and tinier including our attention spans. While I enjoyed a lot of the content as much as the next guy, something really felt off to me. We were all wasting our time with these little bites, as funny or as clever as they were. So instead of going for short videos with the updated Rubin Report, I decided to do hour-long, unedited interviews with no agenda other than good conversation. Old school, à la my broadcasting hero Larry King.

I really had no idea if going bigger at a time when everyone else was going smaller was going to work. But after my first show, an in-depth sit down with neuroscientist and author Sam Harris, I felt I was really onto something. Amazingly enough, the audience agreed, and our YouTube numbers began to explode. Week after week I interviewed interesting people across the cultural and political spectrum and my viewers got to see me learn as they did at home. Going that old school route, just sitting down with someone and actually listening to them instead of trying to destroy them, actually became new school.

Each week as I respectfully sat down with guests with no intention other than to hear what they actually thought, my political evolution began to take hold. My shift from progressive politics of big government, high taxes, and emotions over facts began to fade away and I started to see the world through a clearer lens. Great thinkers like Jordan Peterson, Ben Shapiro, Glenn Beck, Larry Elder, and Thomas Sowell were just a few of the people who helped wake me out of my progressive slumber.

Ideas such as individualism, limited government, personal responsibility, and God-given rights began to not only make sense to me, but to actually spark something within me. The more I explored the notions of freedom and liberty, the further

I wanted to go. And the further I went, the more people tuned in. And the more people who tuned in, the more successful I became. And the more successful I became, the more the rest of my life fell into place. Holy cow, that whole "pursuit of happiness" thing really did make sense!

And actually, it not only made sense, but it is also deeply connected to the other ideas I mentioned just before that. The government can't guarantee your happiness, but it can create the conditions for you to pursue it yourself. Pretty freakin' cool, if you really think about it.

So I kept going. I kept interviewing deep thinkers, I began to say what I thought more and more and the show exploded in a way I never thought imaginable.

These days, I'm fairly certain there are more interview podcasts than human beings on planet Earth. Everyone and their brother seems to have a podcast or a YouTube show. The world's largest podcaster, Joe Rogan, gets millions more views and listens per day than CNN's primetime lineup combined. Alternative voices in politics, sports, gaming, and every other vertical you can think of (and some you can't think of) have come to the forefront of American culture and are shaping old and new generations alike. This incredible democratization of the voices we turn to in order to make sense of the world has opened millions of people up to ideas they would have never heard otherwise. In many ways this concept, new voices debating old ideas (as well as new ones), is the very crux of the crazy world we live in these days. Old media is dying, but like a wounded animal it won't give up without a fight. New media are gaining and flourishing, but now must tackle battles like online censorship and maintaining journalistic integrity.

Alongside this media and technological revolution, a new American generation went from being teenagers to young adults. Of course, I am talking about Gen Z. These are the people who only know a post-internet world, who grew up in the midst of the culture wars, and who carry the entire world in their pocket with an iPhone wherever they go. (Well, I guess we all do that across generations now, but they were doing it while in diapers.)

Gen Z has surpassed the millennials before them as the "It" generation, and they may even surpass the Gen Xers (my generation) as the next pivotal one, because those pesky baby boomers seem to never want to let go. And with the speed Gen Z takes in information, we middle-aged folk may be too slow to stop them.

To me, Gen Z is best described as smart, curious, skeptical, and wide-eyed. Of course there is a split within the generation itself, those who have gone "woke" versus those who have gone more conservative. (Though for my purposes "conservative" in this case only means roughly sane.) While many books, probably way too many books, have been written about the failing of this generation, which is barely off the launching pad, few have been written about the potential, or what to me is the obvious success they will one day attain.

This new, conservative generation of young people are the real rebels in society right now. While their woke counterparts proclaim to be the rebels, the young conservative of today is a rebel in the truest sense. The wokester is rebellious in name only and one need only look at their corporate backing to understand that.

Their conservative friend, if they dare have a friend who thinks differently than they do, is rebellious by their very existence.

They refuse to accept every narrative just because "The Machine" says it's true. They believe in basic truths like the biological reality that there are differences between males and females. They aren't racist and know that America wasn't founded on racism. They have their own religious beliefs but want other people to live as they see fit.

But there is something even deeper going on with them than those ideas. While their woke friends are NPCs—better known as Non-Playable Characters in video games, so-called for their ability to only do repetitive motions over and over rather than act autonomously for themselves—this new breed of non-woke Gen Z young people actually want to take responsibility for their own destiny. They actually relish being active players in the game of life.

I've had the honor of meeting and working with many of these bright young people and I have to tell you they rarely disappoint. Occasionally I even have a twinge of jealousy as I think about how mature they are in their early twenties, something I didn't accomplish until much later, though that's for another book altogether.

As impressed as I am with many of them, a couple manage to stick out.

Isabel and I have crossed paths many times over the past few years. Usually at a Turning Point conference or some other conservative college event. She's interviewed me a handful of times and in the last year I've gotten to know her quite well as, like me, she moved to The Free State of Florida. Full disclosure: Isabel's fiancé Brock is my all-star social media and marketing director, and while hiring him I didn't even know they were dating until several rounds of interviews. Since moving here to Florida, we've gotten to know each other in a more meaningful way (usually over grilled meat and cocktails) as she and Brock begin to take their next steps in life.

The last time Isabel interviewed me was before she had moved to Florida, before Brock was working for me, and before the two of them were engaged. We were at the Turning Point USA annual Student Action Summit in Tampa in the summer of 2022. Isabel approached me as I was finishing up another media hit and kindly asked if I could take some time to sit down with her. I remembered her from a few of our previous chats over the years and was happy to oblige. We went outside to the balcony where her team had set up on a hot and humid Floridian summer day. Not an ideal setup for anyone's forehead shine or hair height, but we did it anyway.

As we sat there in the tall director's chairs waiting for the crew to give us the go, Isabel began to tell me some of the topics she wanted to ask me about. I told her, as I always do with interviewers, that nothing was off limits, and there was no need to tell me what we were going to talk about in advance. I find this often puts interviewers off, because many like to be overly prepared and not stray off script, but I'm always my best when I'm thinking on the fly and responding in real time as candidly as possible.

Isabel gave me a big smile when I said that and we just started talking as organically and naturally as we would off camera. For the next twenty minutes or so she asked me everything from questions about woke culture to COVID policy to leaving the left. I remember exactly what I said when the interview finished and the camera was turned off.

"You're a great interviewer. A really great interviewer."

For as many interviews as I've done over the years, at this point I've probably done just as many, if not more on the other side of the interview. And from being on both sides of the microphone so many times, you learn a little something about what good conversation is all about. And the thing is, it isn't about the obvious stuff. Sure, there are good questions, deep, probing questions, and there are softball, fluff questions. There is tone and demeanor, humor and wit. But actually there is something much more ephemeral that makes a good interviewer or interviewee, for that matter.

It's just sitting there in that moment, in that space, and being present with the person you are with. It's not about judgment or the rush to the next question, it's not about how you look or the camera angle, it's about truly putting the outside world outside and being present in the moment with that other person. It's about actually listening and responding in kind, not trying to get to some predetermined destination. And it was clear to me during and after that interview that Isabel was a master of that, even though she probably didn't even know it. (And maybe still doesn't know it, in which case I've now blown the trick. Sorry Isabel!)

That trait, though, is something that is not only becoming

more and more uncommon in the realm of interviewing, but it's becoming more and more uncommon in the realm of reality. We stare at our phones while we are at the beach. We check emails while out to dinner. We tweet while we are watching a movie. Being present is becoming a rarer and rarer present in and of itself.

And of course, if you are a Gen Zer yourself, you likely never remember a time when being truly present was even a thing. You've grown up with all the distractions, all the gadgets, all the scrolling, and all the clicks and likes. If you go and meet a friend for coffee you stare at your phone for directions to get there, only to wait outside the coffee shop and scroll Instagram mindlessly while you wait for your friend to arrive. Back in my day we used to do something called "people watching." Literally just watching people. That was it. That was the whole thing. They didn't even have filters on. The only blue-haired people we had were the hipsters in the East Village of New York City. They were just real people and you could marvel at them for your own pleasure for as long as you wanted. But I digress.

Being present in a time of the infinite scroll and anchored to reality in a time of dystopian lies, is an unbelievably impressive feat and one Isabel has excelled at. And she hasn't just excelled at it in the political realm, but the personal realm as well, which is why I am proud to call her a colleague but honored to call her a friend.

So whether you are a baby boomer, a Gen Xer, millennial, Gen Zer, or whatever else is after that, I have no doubt that you'll find this book an enjoyable and useful compass as you map out your own political beliefs.

Despite all our modern gadgets and distractions, the human experience always remains constant, and certain ideas stand the test of time. You may not fit into a perfect political box, I know that I certainly do not, but Isabel's candor, thoughtfulness, and humor will help you think for yourself and chart your own course in a world gone mad.

Gen Z may be at the end of the alphabet, but perhaps it's also the start of something else...

Dave Rubin

INTRODUCTION

If I've learned one thing from working as a full-time content creator, it's that *everyone* has an opinion on "youth culture." Rarely,
however, are their opinions rooted in reality. Teenagers and young
adults today are assumed by those who came before us to be a
product of our chaotic civilization—consistently self-absorbed,
steeped in instant gratification, and unable to look up from our
screens to engage with the outside world. We're told we're too
young to comprehend important societal issues, much less care
enough to change them. We're labeled lazy, entitled, apathetic...
you get the picture.

But in our increasingly divided world, Generation Z also is seen
as a prize to be won over. Political and corporate America are racing
to build a youth base, pandering in any way they can to attract new
customers to whatever they're selling, despite fundamentally misunderstanding who this generation is becoming.

For many who came before us, Gen Z is an unrecognizable
demographic. Simply put, we're *different*. We have new means of
communication, unique slang, and different cultural norms. We
dress unconventionally and listen to unusual music. We're moving away from traditional four-year degree programs and toward

unpredictable entrepreneurship. We're living out of suitcases instead of surrounded by white picket fences. We're pushing the boundaries of society as we know it, and it's unnerving pretty much *everyone*.

As a result, I've witnessed American culture push Gen Z aside as unimportant, unimpactful, and unworthy of having a voice for the future of our nation and world. As I'm often called to represent our generation to those who came before us on the news, on the radio, and in print media, this affront to young adults has become a reality I am confronted with on a daily basis.

It may be popular to do, but here's the thing—excommunicating Gen Z is a grave mistake. Teenagers and young adults in America are poised to become the single largest age demographic in our nation's history, packing a bigger punch politically and culturally than anyone who has come before us. We're already the likeliest generation to speak up about the things we believe in and the likeliest generation to boycott companies we disagree with, according to the BBC. We aren't waiting for permission to do things our own way.

Gen Z is redefining cultural norms for ourselves through online advocacy, entrepreneurship, boots-on-the-ground activism, and political impact at earlier and earlier ages. Today's 12- to 25-year-olds may be young, but we aren't apathetic, and we aren't waiting for permission from older generations to make culture our own. We're rejecting the prescribed boxes of society we were presented with and building our own destinies. As a result, in the world of content creation and politics I often work in, people commonly refer to Generation Z as "Generation Free."

My hope is that this book dispels the "Gen Z is the enemy" narrative, unpacking the lies that our society has identified with Gen Z and reintroducing you to the promise of the next generation. Despite what you may hear on the news or see scrolling through your social media feed, there is no reason to have anything but hope for the future with my generation climbing into the driver's seat of culture. We're hungry for major cultural change, rejecting the cultural norms that have devolved America into all-out chaos.

We are the end of the alphabet—and perhaps the end of life as we know it—but that may not be such a bad thing after all.

More importantly, I hope this book serves as an opportunity for change. The powerful one-sided narrative Gen Zers face daily from every pillar of culture—our schools, our jobs, our churches, our entertainment, our politicians, and more—that we must embrace authoritarianism and sacrifice our liberty at the altar of big government is rarely effectively challenged. At the very least, attempts to challenge this narrative for Gen Z often come across as preachy or lecturing a "degenerate youth culture" about returning to the "good ol' days." No longer can we operate in a cultural conversation that treats young adults as "lesser than" if we want to change the heartbeat of our nation. We must provide my generation a venue for discovery, for challenging conversation, for a change of perspective—or face the consequences of those in power's continued quelling of young voices.

In the 2020s, we are in the midst of the greatest cultural tug-of-war our nation has perhaps ever faced. The future of what it means to be an American—and even what it means to be free—remains in question as competing entities ferociously battle for the soul of our country. Today, every aspect of our lives ultimately boils down to a controversial, political statement—from who we follow online to what brand of underwear we purchase. Our leaders call for unity but simultaneously spew divisive hatred whenever they get the chance. We're falling prisoner to the constantly changing demands of cancel culture, when all we simply want is to be *free*.

As the wheels continue spinning at an increasing rate into absurdity, the need for the conversations held within these pages grows with each passing moment. This book was written on bumpy airplane rides flying coast to coast, on rural back roads driving across the nation, and on college campuses in every region of the country. While most manuscripts take years to put together, I hurried to write this book to counter the frantic pace of those seeking to destroy our nation in its entirety. As I've continued to engage in the ever-changing nature of American culture as a content creator, public speaker, political commentator, and author, it's become increasingly apparent to me how badly our nation needs a change of pace toward sanity, goodness, and truth. This change can no longer exist in "someday" as a far-off dream, but as you read these words in this very moment.

In an era demanding a cultural revolution to achieve meaningful common ground and a hopeful step forward, one unique generation stands poised to make that change. Empowering Gen Z to continue rejecting the destruction of our culture and build a stronger future in coalition with those who came before us are the keys to a future of promise—one in which we *all* become "Generation Free."

CHAPTER 1

doomed or chosen?

Recently, I conducted a poll on my Instagram story asking my followers to use a single word to describe my generation, Generation Z. Instantly, dozens of responses came flooding in, and unsurprisingly, the dichotomy between Gen Z's understanding of ourselves and the opinions of those who came before us could not have been more obvious. Common answers from my millennial, Gen X, and baby boomer followers painted a picture of an entitled generation who will certainly manifest the utter destruction of our society. Anxious. Doomed. Weak. Confused. Delusional. Suckers. Zombies. Immature. Unaccountable. Self-obsessed. Immoral. Misguided. Spoiled. Egocentric. Fake. Victims. Dum (spelled incorrectly—ha!). Indoctrinated. Broken. Doomed. Lost. *Fucked.*

Incredibly, the same question posed to my peers elicited a starkly different response: Motivated. Searching. Curious. Entrepreneurial. Worthy. Ready. Passionate. *Chosen.*

Asking Americans to describe my generation in a single word has become one of my favorite questions, both online and in person while giving speeches or engaging in conversation with people all over the country. Far more often than not, I have discovered that those older than myself could not hold more contempt for young people today. Not only are we different in our generational values from our parents and grandparents, but we're rapidly changing the nature of our way of life (for the worse, they'll be glad to tell you). We've become the boogeyman for the destruction of America, as silly as it sounds, and are not to be trusted, empowered, or uplifted. Instead, we ought to be cast aside, quieted down, and told to wait our turn.

Meanwhile, ask any Gen Zer to describe our own generation, and you'll find an optimistic, charismatic, empathetic collection of voices that couldn't be more different from the angry socialists those older than us describe us to be. We share a collective hope in the ability of our peers to change culture for the better, even if our predecessors insist on condemning and chastising us for being young. While others view us as hyper-individualistic and self-obsessed, we share a societal empathy to take care of one another and build a stronger future.

In 2024, it's become impossible to utter the term "Generation Z" without eliciting a visceral reaction from virtually everyone in the United States. Most older people seem to find my generation of teenagers and young adults to be migraine inducing, worthy of condemnation, and solely responsible for ruining America as our society devolves further from reality. Living in a culture shaped by moral relativism and disdain for the truth, Gen Z is often blamed for every crazy headline and viral social media post. We're thought of as the generation who voluntarily ate Tide Pods and would rather dance in crop tops on TikTok than make a profound impact on society. Of course, there *are* a handful of idiots who gave us that reputation in the first place, but the overwhelming narrative has ballooned to characterize tens of millions of teenagers and young adults as uneducated degenerates with a disdain for all things good. After all, it's easy to blame the destruction of society on a bunch of juvenile morons who always have their eyes glued to a phone screen.

Spending so much of my time working in politics has revealed to me just how much this abrogating attitude has been amplified in recent years. Politicians, commentators, and activist organizations alike continue to label Gen Z as a threat to American liberty, morally bankrupt, malicious in our supposed intent to destroy Western society, and just plain *stupid.* High-profile voices from both sides of the political aisle have chastised my generation in order to rally their base, stirring fear in others that life as we know it in America is sure to become extinct if Gen Z isn't confronted, indoctrinated, or manipulated to vote for their causes. We've become pawns in a 4D chess game for political control, and we've had enough.

It's often said today that we live in two different Americas—largely because of the increasing partisan divide pulling at the seams of society. Our media, entertainment, education, religion, friendships, shopping habits, and everything else have become politically driven in the 2020s. The music we listen to, the chocolate bars we eat, and the video games we play have evolved past a fun pastime or treat to enjoy into a jarring partisan statement sure to incite the cancel culture mob to come after us. Red states and blue states no longer have much, or truly anything, in common as we drift farther apart along the political spectrum. Some (even those in Congress) are calling for a national divorce, encouraging states with overwhelming political majorities to consider seceding from the Union entirely. We're told the contrast between Left and Right has become so absolute, we've moved beyond any hope for reconciliation or finding common ground. Instead, anyone who votes or thinks differently than we do is purely evil—no ifs, ands, or buts about it.

While our partisan divide is certainly cause for widespread concern, I have come to believe in recent years that we have another (and perhaps even more concerning) chasm in America than that of Left versus Right. The widening canyon between America's next great generation, Gen Z, and those who came before us should be sounding alarms all over the country. Instead, we far too often choose to add gasoline to the fire of division and threaten to destroy hope for the future of our nation entirely, hell-bent on remaining generationally divided rather than finding opportunities to come together.

The truth is, we *do* live in two different Americas—one characterized by those longing for a return to the "good ol' days" before the insanity of the 2020s; the other understanding the need to move forward to a stronger future than the present. The world against Gen Z, or Gen Z against the world, depending on how you look at it. We've become so obsessed with societal division that we're voluntarily feeding into it instead of finding the humanity in one another. Young people roll their eyes at the "boomer" mentality they think fails to understand our generation's way of life, while older generations bemoan the demise of the "once great" society they loved growing up in with the dawn of a new age.

While this divide is growing at an unprecedented rate today, it's easy to forget that older generations having disdain for youth culture is not a new phenomenon—it's something humanity has been doing for thousands of years. Older people's complaints against their younger counterparts' way of life are baked into the foundation of human nature, all over the world. Peter O'Connor, an Australian professor at Queensland University of Technology, shared with the BBC's Katie Bishop in an article called "Are Younger Generations Truly Weaker Than Older Ones?" that generational disdain is not a new concept. He believes "the tendency for adults to disparage the character of youth has been happening for centuries."[1]

In reality, the generational divide isn't confined to angry baby boomers' animosity toward selfie-taking, avocado-toast eating millennials or TikToking Gen Zers, but has existed since the time of the Ancient Greeks. Even boomers were denounced by their parents in the 1960s as "irresponsible hippies," psychology professor Alison Gopnik reminds us in the *Wall Street Journal*.[2] Turns out, the cyclical psychology of looking down upon your children's generation has been repeated through all of human history, something she calls the "kids these days" effect. Each generation isn't deteriorating into degeneracy the way we often believe, but our perspectives shaped by our unique generational values continue creating the same disdain, decade after decade.

It doesn't help today that our various generations rarely intermix. We move out on our own as early as possible in search of independence from Mom and Dad. We're surrounded largely by our peers for our college and young professional years, rarely interacting with those much older than us. We visit our grandparents and elderly relatives only on occasion, sparingly having the opportunity for cross-generational dialogue.

Our isolation from one another has catalyzed intergenerational warfare on social media, marked by "Ok, boomer" and "Gen Z is destroying America" comments scattered all over cyberspace. The same parent-to-child generational gap that exists between baby boomers and millennials, spurring meme-worthy internet warfare between the two, has spawned between Gen Zers and our Gen X parents—so much so that we're now calling our parents "The Karen Generation," as BuzzFeed noted. Comments flood our social media feeds teeming with frustration like "Gen X are just out here yelling at fast food and retail employees."[3]

While it's certainly good fodder to chuckle at and repost to our own feeds, the sad reality is America's handling of intergenerational dialogue is missing the mark. We're losing out on the opportunity to learn from one another, have hope for one another, and rely on one another. Instead, we battle for relevancy and control over a society that is slipping away from all of us.

America's disdain for Gen Z has become one of the most common topics I am asked to cover as a political commentator and public speaker who is facilitating dialogue with baby boomers, Gen X, and millennials about what they're fundamentally misunderstanding regarding today's teenagers and young adults. While we've become the boogeyman for the destruction of America for those who came before us, the truth is, someone *else* had to build the messed-up, upside-down, unrecognizable world we grew up in. We may be the recipients of participation trophies, of moral relativism, and of subjective truth—but those who raised us carefully constructed the America we live in today throughout our formative years to be characterized as such. Our unprecedented levels of anxiety and depression, our increasing political divide, our inability to define gender, and more have arisen as the end result of an America in steady decline since the birth of our generation, and sadly, we've been educated to accelerate her demise.

While our predecessors point the finger of blame right at us, Gen Z has been isolated from active participation in the national conversation for far too long. With each passing year, Western values and society are threatened by those with malicious intent to destroy the foundation of our nation forevermore, and it's going to take all of us to build a stronger future for every generation to come after the "end of the alphabet." While those older than us have increasingly strong opinions about how terrible my generation is, a stronger path forward has to begin with empowering Gen Z to lead, knowing that it will inevitably be us tasked with directing the trajectory of this crazy experiment we call America into tomorrow.

Genuinely, I understand the concern expressed by boomers, Gen Xers, and even some millennials surrounding the ever-changing nature of reality with each passing day. It's easy to assume that the young, loud, larger-than-life kids who came after you are to blame, but we all have a role and responsibility in acknowledging how we have allowed America to crumble this far, and how we can rebuild our foundation before it's too late. Placing the blame on Gen Z is a misguided attempt to abdicate this obligation, and if we are to have a country that we're proud to call home again, it's time to stop the cycle of generational slander that's rarely based in reality. In truth, as you'll soon discover, there is no reason to have anything but hope for Gen Z as we make our generational mark on history.

In early 2023, I had the unique opportunity to appear as a guest on an increasingly viral dating show, the *Whatever* podcast, in Santa Barbara, California. Throughout the weeks leading up to the appearance, I engaged with dozens of clips from the show on social media involving a wide variety of opinions on some of the most important topics of our time, from hookup culture to gender theory and everything in between. Sometimes, girls would become so outraged by traditional values and commonsense ideas that they'd dramatically storm off set or start yelling at their co-panelists—but more often than not, genuine conversation that society has deemed "taboo" was taking place. In a refreshing change of pace, people were learning to comfortably disagree with one another while continuing to expand their own viewpoints and opinions, and as a viewer, I was hooked.

I've never been much for trash TV or reality shows—in fact, to this day I've only ever seen one episode of *The Bachelor* franchise and have never watched *Keeping Up with the Kardashians*. I did have a special affinity for *Dance Moms* growing up as a competitive dancer myself, but truly, the *Whatever* podcast has been my first experience indulging in a guilty pleasure. I often find myself scrolling through their TikTok account, eyes glued to the panelists sharing their craziest dating experiences, which made my eyes widen. Knowing my status as a happily engaged Catholic 25-year-old was so dramatically different from their usual lineup, I was ecstatic to present my point of view, and likely get some great viral social media content out of the opportunity.

I showed up to the studio on a rainy spring day to meet my co-panelists prior to the show, and at first glance I was convinced I would have a hard time articulating the things I so passionately stand for. At first blush, the girls I would be appearing with couldn't be more different from myself. We represented a rainbow of racial diversity, came from all different parts of the country, and were all at different stages in our dating and relationship lives. When I say "different," though, I really mean it: while I was an engaged, conservative content creator and author, other girls appearing included a recovering sex addict and even an OnlyFans creator/stripper/porn star. Literally.

The conversationalist in me lit up at the opportunity to speak to different people than I normally have a chance to interact with, and I'd be lying if I said I wasn't excited about some potential backlash I would be able to post on my social media.

As we pushed through introductions on the five-hour-long podcast conversation, my eyes widened when I heard what several of the women sitting around me had to say: one loved having sugar daddies, one had slept with over 150 men, and most could not be more different in their walks of life from myself. As the conversation evolved and turned toward dating culture and American culture at large, though, I was even more floored to discover that *every single one* of these women agreed with my perspective: whatever we are doing in modern culture is not working and is setting Gen Z up for failure. I certainly didn't see *that* coming.

Over an hour into our conversation, I asked the group if they believed that modern feminism was a problem. Immediately, a chorus of voices responded with shocking testimony (from a group that pretty obviously looked like your average modern feminists):

"Yes. Feminism is a cult."

"It's literally a supremacist group."

"Feminism is just crazy. It's rooted in brokenness."

My face immediately broke into a wide smile (as I'm sure you can see on video somewhere) as I took in the environment. Turns out, these women I had profoundly misjudged, and who likely still disagree with me on a whole host of cultural issues, all understood intimately just how much post-modern culture is lying to our generation. The conversation again found common ground about how much we'd all been negatively impacted by years of hormonal birth control, with nearly everyone around the table saying how glad they were they quit. Several women shared their viewpoints on how broken our rampant hookup culture had become, treating women (and men, too!) as transactional commodities rather than someone to be loved and cherished. Shockingly, every woman sitting around the table agreed they would date a pro-life man if given the opportunity and reflected their belief that abortion culture had profoundly impacted modern relationships for the worse.

Toward the end of the show, I made an observation: here I was in a small loft studio in California surrounded by people I ordinarily would never have had the opportunity to engage with, covering some of the most important subjects impacting our culture and generational identity today. To my absolute shock, every one of us deeply, passionately believed that modern culture is. Not. Working. Full stop.

From the body-and-brain-altering birth control pills seemingly every doctor in America is pushing the women of my generation to take, to the all-too-common transactional hookup culture we all have been impacted by, even to the entire movement of modern feminism: culture has set Gen Z up for failure, heartbreak, and loss. No matter where we came from, where we were at in our relationship journey, or our political views that threatened to divide us, we universally came together to affirm a need to take America in a different direction—regardless of what those with the loudest voices in society have to say about it.

I realized in retrospect that I had fallen victim to the increasingly powerful divisiveness propagated against Gen Z and had made up my mind about the girls I would be speaking with before we uttered a word—even as a Gen Zer myself! While I didn't get many potentially viral clips for TikTok or Instagram out of the experience, I gained something far more valuable from the conversation: the powerful reminder that Gen Z has the capacity and desire to come together in the midst of this dark, seemingly hopeless cultural moment and lay the foundation for a stronger future.

Our generation has perhaps been confronted with facing more adversity than any generation of Americans before us in several decades—which also makes us uniquely equipped and prepared to lead as our nation faces a breaking point in where we go from here. In the midst of uncertainty, turmoil, and all-out fear for what the future holds, I am reminded daily that every generation was intentionally created by God for the right time and place.

The Old Testament book of Esther tells the gripping tale of a young Jewish woman who finds favor with the king of the time to later become queen, risking her life to save her people from utter destruction after those in political power urge violence and destruction against the Jews.[4] It's easily one of my favorite stories in the Bible, and reminds people from all over the world on a daily basis that no matter the hurdles we face or the adversity we are born into, we have the capacity to lead simply because we were born into this time and place with intentionality from the God of the Universe. Esther 4:14 outlines this simple truth so powerfully: "For if you remain silent at this time, relief and deliverance for the Jews will arise from another place, but you and your father's family will perish. And who knows but that you have come to your royal position *for such a time as this*?"[5]

For the vast majority of societal associations, you have a say in the matter of who you choose to hitch your wagon to. You can choose what group of friends you associate with, what school you attend, what clubs you join. You can choose which company to work for or which neighborhood to live in. You can choose what religion to practice and political party to support. Interestingly, though, you *can't* choose which generation you belong to. You don't choose it—it chooses you.

Through regularly traversing the nation, engaging in dialogue from the heart of dozens of college campuses, and spending far too much time online, I have come to believe that Gen Z is exactly who America desperately needs in 2024 and beyond to reclaim our nation from the brink of destruction. While others remain silent in the midst of truth's perishing, we are embracing the call to lead. Despite the powerful narrative of our predecessors spelling our inevitable doom with Gen Z at the helm, I believe we are instead chosen to lead through this uncertain, unrecognizable time. After all, we were made for such a time as this.

CHAPTER 2

the upside down

I'll never forget the first time I was told I was "too young" to be speaking onstage at a political event—that being in my early twenties, despite everything I may have accomplished up to that point, didn't give me enough "life experience" to be an expert on just about any topic, let alone modern politics. At first, I chuckled, assuming this was a poorly delivered joke aimed at making me laugh. When I realized this person (an audience member at a conference I'd been asked to speak at) was serious, I was stunned. While I had always been encouraged to make my voice heard, no matter my age, I soon discovered that many in American culture continue to struggle with lifting young voices simply because they are young. It seems the price of admission to speak to others about our nation's future wasn't my accomplishments or who I was as a person, but instead the number of years I have lived on earth and how many birthdays I've celebrated—as if that was the only way to prove my qualification on any subject.

The problem with this viewpoint is that we've consistently conflated "life experience" and wisdom with age, assuming that a higher number of years under our belts automatically grants us acumen we lacked as younger beings. In truth, wisdom and insight most often flourish as a result of our *experiences* rather than our years. Most often, you gain experience over time with age, but there are countless stories of courageous young people who have overcome mountains of adversity and undertaken experiences those decades older than them may never face.

There are, in fact, 20-year-olds walking among us with more wisdom than some 80-year-olds (looking at you, United States Congress), but those with the loudest voices and most powerful societal roles would never admit it. Though teenagers and young adults today are generally identified as ignorant, I would argue the wealth of experiences Generation Z has undertaken throughout our relatively short existence throughout the last twenty-six years have provided a unique perspective from which to view the world, making us much more equipped to lead than many would assume. In reality, our formative years have been a journey of uncharted territory for humanity, raising new questions about ethics, warfare, technology, politics, faith, relationships, and even gender that my generation will inevitably be forced to find an answer to—ready, or not.

Gen Z, Who Are We?

Gen Z today is made up of teenagers and young adults born between 1997 and 2012, growing up in perhaps the most complicated time in modern history. From our conception, we were thrust into a timeline marred by chaos. Born in the confusion of

Y2K, the technology boom of the 2000s laid the foundation for America's first generation of "digital natives." The oldest among us remember a time before iPhones and tablets, playing outside on a carefree snow day with our friends and lacking parental supervision while navigating blocky Game Boy consoles as "complicated" technology. I will always remember the day when my mom tossed me her hand-me-down shiny pink brick of an iPod—one of the first models—and I spent hours discovering which way to move my thumb in a circle to change the volume. Innovating an entire new world of technology never before seen by humanity became a mesmerizing chapter of our history, which, incredibly, the youngest members of Gen Z can't even attempt to relate to.

The age gap between myself and my youngest sister is roughly five years, which doesn't seem like a lot, until you factor in the perspective that I didn't have a childhood defined by social media and texting until well into middle school—while she barely, if at all, remembers a time without Instagram filters and group texts. Particularly young Gen Zers still in their teen years likely have never experienced reality with landline telephones or VHS tapes (and, frighteningly, may barely remember DVDs). In early 2023, our beloved American Girl dolls even got a new addition to the lineup of "historical characters," twins Nicki and Isabel (Is she me? I hope so!), who were young kids in 1999, outfitted with accessories like a desktop computer with a mix CD, a landline phone, plastic blowup chair for their room, and a late-'90s Pizza Hut box set. Things have changed so quickly, it seems, that the archetypal items of my earliest memories are now viewed through a "historical" lens by 2023 standards. The dolls' launch, honestly, made me feel 105 instead of 25, but in the digital age, time seems to move at warp speed.

Younger Gen Zers are interfacing with technology in a much more complicated and contrived manner than the carefree, fun era of exploration us "born-in-the-late-1900s" Gen Zers did (yes, they actually say that on TikTok). My younger peers have spent far more time interacting with their friends through a screen than hanging out before a high school football game. Their first sexual experiences aren't happening with awkward kissing or sneaking out; they're happening through screens watching pornography or chatting on dating apps. They can hop in self-driving Ubers already on the roads or put their Teslas on autopilot on the freeway. It's possible for them to write entire dissertations using a one-sentence prompt through artificial intelligence, and suddenly the technology-driven utopia that glossed the big screen through our favorite Marvel movies has become our reality.

No idea is too impossible. Literally—we're 3D-printing human organs. We're building artificial lab-grown meat. You can check out at the store with the swipe of your *palm* through biometric payment. Tech entrepreneurs are ideating brain-implant microchips, putting our computers into our heads. We've made imagination and innovation synonymous, which has also opened our eyes to an entirely new reality facing the question "Just because you can, *should* you?" While we didn't create the world we're growing up in, we will be the ones left in the driver's seat—never mind the fact that no one has driven on this road before. Technology and digital innovation have dumped a massive obligation into the lap of my generation. While navigating the uncharted territory of our new millennium, how are we going to responsibly safeguard ourselves from crossing the line? When will we know if our culture at large has transformed from a safe haven to a perilous battleground?

The oldest among us were babies and toddlers amid the chaos of the terrorist attacks on September 11, 2001 (most weren't even born yet), which forever changed the nature of conflict and warfare at the global level from the time of our infancy. As we watched our parents' eyebrows creased with worry and eyes glued to television screens, it was easy to understand that humanity had entered uncharted territory, but we were consistently reminded of newfound dangers close to home ourselves, too. Since elementary school, we've regularly practiced our defensive strategy for school shootings, dreading the seemingly inevitable day such an atrocity would affect our own school community (or sadly, even our grocery stores, movie theaters, or churches, where we ordinarily always felt safe). Incredibly, despite adults we trusted saying we surely would be safe, this strategy meant we were told to sit quietly in the corner of our classrooms cowering in fear as sitting targets for the "bad guy" we were convinced would become our assailants. Never mind, of course, the inconvenient reality that every expert has concluded, that only makes us more likely to be injured or killed. Constantly prepared for the worst, even our favorite books and movies as children and teenagers centered around dystopian futures, from the apocalyptic setting of *The Hunger Games* to the communistic execution of unwanted citizens in *The Giver.*

From our infancy, the world we've grown up in has flipped upside down over and over again, from wonder to doom and back again. We've gone from 1990s-era marked by hit sitcoms and kids playing outside on their neighborhood summer streets to a violently turbulent early-2000s. Forever marked by the September 11 attacks, the earliest years of our memories were shaped when the generation before us was shipped to the other side of the globe for the "war on terror." Our young childhood was characterized by the merging of politics and culture in the "hope and change" era of the Obama administration, coupled with a devastating economy that drove our parents out of their jobs and even out of our homes.

Approaching the 2010s, our childhood became a chapter of Disney Channel original movies, Sillybandz bracelets, and YA-fantasy novel series. It seemed as soon as we started listening to One Direction and logging onto Club Penguin, the world transformed again into a time where our entire reality began to exist through a screen. The era of social media that was once a singular platform to "friend" people you'd lost touch with exploded into the rise of Instagram, Snapchat, Tumblr, Twitter, and more all at once. As Instagram climbed the app charts during my sophomore year of high school, it became far more culturally important to regularly post everything you were doing to make your life more "artsy" while carefully choosing VSCO filters that made your existence appear uniform in your feed. As if trying to impress your peers wasn't already stressful enough in high school, now we had the added pressure of a flawless online presence that started to define who we were offscreen, too.

Watching TV began to transform from once-a-week live episodes to streaming on-demand, feeding into the instant gratification slowly starting to define every aspect of society. Even our first debit cards were managed through online banking platforms, much to our parents' shock and horror. Shopping stopped being long days at the mall, trying on new clothes for school or nervously hanging out with your first crush and your friends—it happened through punching the numbers of a credit card into your Amazon profile where something would be delivered within mere hours.

Our curriculum started to rapidly evolve, too—suddenly, graduation requirements didn't just center around typing 100 words per minute, but included coding, web design, and even app development. Computer science was no longer centered around how to work a computer; it became how we could manipulate and change technology into whatever we could possibly imagine. I started high school with a heavy backpack full of scribbled-on notebooks and thick textbooks and finished with sleek mandatory iPads, where we stored all our notes and textbooks alike digitally. Personally, I preferred the messy scribbles on old-school notebooks and flipping the pages of my bulky textbooks, but perhaps that's just the old soul bookworm in me.

The stark dichotomy between innocent exploration of what a new world could become in the twenty-first century as young children, and what it quickly became within less than two decades, is enough to baffle any mind. How crazy to think the internet, a fun new universe to watch YouTube videos or log onto Webkinz, quickly became a necessary and required skill not only to graduate high school but to thrive as an adult in the modern world. And don't you worry, we've always had our parents to remind us they didn't have the luxury of Google or even Microsoft Word to write their papers back in the Stone Ages.

The Best Chapter of Our Lives?

Throughout our formative years, we daydreamed about what it would finally be like to move away and go to college. Perhaps the most iconic American experience narrated through our favorite feel-good movies and our parents' photo albums was promised to be the best time of our lives. Packing for our dorm, we listened to Mom and Dad recount stories through glistening, wistful eyes about fraternity parties and football games, sure we'd feel the same someday with the next great chapter of our lives kicking off adulthood. We'd probably meet our best friends for life, our future spouses, and become inspired and prepared for our careers. We were sure to have our perspectives challenged, expose our minds to new ways of thinking, and ask the big questions through passionate debate over beer and pizza or in lecture-style classrooms...right?

Wrong.

Gen Z's experience in higher education could not be more fundamentally at odds with what college and higher education at large are supposed to be. Rather than being exposed to a multitude of worldviews and perspectives or be challenged in our own values—you know, being *educated*—we're being indoctrinated to buy into a singular ideology with a lockstep rigor and nearly religious adherence. Academia today is no longer about providing a Renaissance education, but shaping a generation where everyone looks different, but thinks exactly the same.

When our parents attended college in the '80s, political view-points or partisan affiliations were rarely a component of the university experience. Politics was rarely something that defined their curriculum, their friendships, or their opportunities for success, and even when it did come up, classrooms were venues for dialogue instead of angry intolerance. As I've often heard my parents recount, even in their law school environment, politics was merely a subject of theoretical discussion rather than a professor's playbook for right versus wrong. In the 1989-1990 school year, a national study found that 42% of college faculty identified as being on the left, 40% identified as moderate, and 18% identified as being on the right. Hardly 50-50, but a multitude of viewpoints were represented among professors, which were incorporated well into learning environments to expose students to a variety of perspectives and challenge one's opinions.

Fast forward to the 2016-2017 school year, smack dab in the middle of my college experience: the same study found that 60% of college faculty identified themselves as either Far Left or liberal, while just 12% self-identified as conservative or Far Right. Within just three decades, the ratio of leftist to conservative college faculty members had more than doubled.[1] Ask anyone my age who recently graduated, or a student currently enrolled in college today—it shows. Not only does this shocking statistic exist, but our professors are acting upon it to shove their personal ideology into our curriculum at every possible opportunity.

At America's most prestigious universities, where Gen Z has been promised to receive the most well-rounded, Renaissance-style education possible, the ratio grows to a shockingly one-sided

23

status. Leading up to the controversial 2016 election, for example, 96% of political donations from Harvard University professors went to Democrats, according to The College Fix.[2] In an interview the same year with Fox News, Georgetown Law professor Nicholas Quinn Rosenkranz shared this about his teaching experience: "It is a shame that our greatest universities have become ideologically monolithic. At many of these schools, including Georgetown Law School, most students will graduate without ever laying eyes on a single Republican professor."[3] Having taken several classes at Georgetown Law myself during my graduate school enrollment, I certainly can confirm.

Naturally, the overwhelming one-sided narrative on campus has dramatically impacted our student experience. In 2018, Yale University conducted a national survey of 800 undergraduate students with shocking results—more than half of them reported they "often" were intimidated by their peers, and 62% of those surveyed who identified as conservative "often" felt silenced on campus. This is hardly surprising, given the outright intolerance we often see on college campuses toward traditional Western values these days. What's truly surprising about Yale's findings, however, is that 53% of moderate and liberal students alike surveyed *also* reported feeling silenced and uncomfortable about sharing their thoughts and challenging the status quo on campus.[4] We've created a culture of lockstep authoritarianism inside our institutions of higher education—unless you embrace the trajectory of the radical Left, you will be ostracized and silenced for your viewpoints, whether you're counterculturally conservative or not.

The singular narrative perpetuated as "truth" by the "experts" Gen Z is supposed to trust to broaden our horizons— our professors—has become so overpowering that we feel out of place sharing our own ideas *at all* in an academic environment—even if we agree with our faculty. Truly, the pillar of American culture most dedicated to progressing our society forward has begun regressing us to a realm of censorship, intolerance, and fear. Sounds like the opposite of a free society in any historical description.

In my own undergraduate experience studying Biomedical Sciences at Colorado State University (hardly politically polarizing, one would think), we didn't focus solely on the pursuit of objective truth...what *science*, especially in academia, is supposed to be all about. Instead, we spent much more time than I ever could have imagined being lectured to by our professors on their opinions surrounding border walls, the First Amendment to the Constitution, or the evil orange guy who had just been elected to sit in the Oval Office. We spent weeks learning every detail of human development in my physiology course, down to when fingerprints formed and a child can start to feel pain in utero, only to be told before the exam that abortion was not the end of a genetically unique human life. We discovered the countless complicated efforts being undertaken to fight and potentially cure cancer in cellular bio, only to be told that government-run health care was really the only way we could ever accomplish something meaningful in the fight. In biology, we actually had a multiple-choice exam question asking about the origins of the universe in which the correct answer choice was (a) a spontaneous eruption billions of years ago starting with a single cell, and the *wrong* answer choice was (b) the universe was created by God. So much room for debate and discovery! *Not.*

I often found myself on campus surrounded by tens of thousands of people who watched the same television shows I did, listened to the same music I did, went to the same football games I did, but didn't share a single one of my values. How was it possible that at a campus of 33,000 students I could feel so isolated and alone? In the back of my mind I knew this couldn't possibly be true, but it often felt this way from the heart of my intolerant environment.

When I finally reached a breaking point and was tired of keeping my head down and mouth shut (it may surprise you to discover I've never been one to sit down and shut up; shocker, I know), I decided to start a club for political dialogue and conservative values. Alone. That meant setting up a rickety folding table in the heart of campus and distributing buttons that read "Socialism Sucks" or posters reading "Women don't need the government to succeed." Frequently on the receiving end of dirty looks or "FUCK YOU!"s from my peers and professors alike, I constantly felt it would be easy to throw in the towel and just get through college without causing a stir, but I decided to forge ahead anyway. After all, if I was feeling isolated and alone, statistically others were, too.

The next few years were characterized by death threats and threats of violence or rape from members of my community, F's on papers and assignments from professors who didn't like that I had invited Dennis Prager or Candace Owens to speak on campus, and the loss of too many friends to count who were content to follow the crowd into authoritarianism. I even had the address to the one-bedroom apartment where I lived just off campus alone doxxed online after giving an interview to the local newspaper. It seemed a local Antifa activist was upset with the conversations I was having on campus exposing my peers to a new political perspective—how dare anyone do that on a public college campus, right?

When Turning Point USA founder Charlie Kirk came to speak to our organization, attracting 700+ students and faculty from campus who were genuinely interested in broadening their perspectives and challenging their viewpoints, protests raged outside our student center. I was tasked with repeatedly meeting with the CSU Police Department during the weeks leading up to Charlie's visit after chatter had been picked up online by Antifa, who planned on shutting down the gathering. The Colorado National Guard was deployed to our campus and set up sniper stations on the computer science building and concrete barricades in the heart of campus to prevent angry, anarchic protesters from potentially driving cars through the student body. Intellectual diversity was so intolerable that the local police department was genuinely convinced lives were at risk—maybe even mine—for daring to suggest we have a thought-provoking conversation *about free speech*. On a *public college campus*. How fascist of me, I guess.

Incredibly, despite the backlash, we quickly became one of the largest clubs on campus with hundreds of members—conservative, libertarian, even liberal—who were deeply hungry for meaningful, rigorous, challenging dialogue and education they weren't getting in their classrooms. Thousands of students and faculty alike showed up to our events with nationally renowned speakers, craving a challenge to the singular perspective they were forced to comply with inside the walls of their classrooms. Many even quietly approached me on campus from time to time, expressing sentiments of gratitude. "You don't know me, and I can't publicly support your organization or you, but thank you for what you're doing," became a common whisper accompanied by a smile around campus. Never in my wildest dreams did I anticipate the thought-provoking, intellectually stimulating college experience I was promised by my high school teachers, parents, and older cousins wouldn't exist, thanks to my university administration. Instead, because a 19-year-old had the passion for genuine education and dialogue her academics refused to foster on campus, she was doing the administration's job for them.

What felt like an out-of-this world experience on the front lines of a battle for the future of American culture headquartered at Colorado State University, of all places, appears tame compared to what most college students willing to break the mold today must deal with. Gen Zers who dare to challenge the narrative on campus face countless death threats, physical assaults, failed grades, lost opportunities, and isolation from their peers every day on virtually every college campus in America. For what? Raising their hand to challenge their professor. Writing about why free speech matters in a political science course. Inviting a right-of-center speaker or classical liberal to speak on campus instead of Angela Davis or Bernie Sanders. Having the audacity to suggest God created the universe instead of a spontaneous eruption of life. Most sadly, even being willing to have a conversation with those they disagree with in the first place.

The great irony of our college experience as a generation is how ill equipped we've emerged to tackle the challenges of a constantly changing world on graduation day, despite becoming the most widely educated generation in history. Gen Z has found ourselves thrust into adulthood, "the real world," so to speak, unprepared for genuine discussion with people different from ourselves, scared to challenge our rigid worldviews built within the four walls of our college lecture halls, and shocked to discover that there may not even be professions available in the fields of study we were encouraged to pursue in the name of academic progressivism. Turns out being a gender studies major was great for social clout on campus but isn't good for much other than going back to school forever—shocking, I know.

How ironic that throughout our entire educational journey, we've been told by our teachers, guidance counselors, professors, and even parents how lucky we are to live in this generation—that there are no more cultural barriers to be whoever we want to be. That if we can dream it, we can do it...yet we are more rigid in our educational culture than ever. If you dare to think differently on an American college campus, you can kiss any one of those dreams good-bye.

A New Normal

It's often said that every year gets faster as you live it—that your twentieth year feels significantly shorter than your tenth, and according to our parents, after 25, we'll blink and suddenly be 50. This once universal human experience all came crashing down for us as the world slammed on the brakes to a standstill in the spring of 2020 upon the arrival of COVID-19. It's crazy to think, by the way, that a string of five letters that were seemingly meaningless before became a word that turned the world upside down. What began as an extended spring break on our high school and college calendars quickly became a vehicle for a complete transformation of our reality. Overnight, we were cut off from our friends, family, classmates, and coworkers as those in power pleaded with us to stay in our homes to "slow the spread" of a virus the world knew nothing about. In an instant, our most basic nonverbal communication—smiling—was cloistered behind a mandatory piece of fabric permanently affixed to our faces, and it often felt like our generation and society at large may never smile freely again.

The "experts" told us to sit back and simply "trust the science," which baffled me as a trained scientist. How could we have transformed so substantially and so quickly to a time where "the science" wasn't about waiting for the research results or asking the big questions, but instead trusting the opinion of one guy on TV who dubbed *himself* "THE science" investigating a virus we've never encountered before? How could that mean cornering an entire generation into mandatory mask wearing (putting ourselves at risk for other diseases and infections) and injections hardly studied for a virus that had nearly impossible odds of even making young people notably sick, let alone threatening our lives? We learned the hard way quickly, though—sit down, shut up, and don't question any of it at the risk of being censored, humiliated, and deplatformed (only to find out years later that everyone raising concerns about treatment protocols, mask effectiveness, etc., turned out to be right as soon as the media began reporting it themselves...in 2023).

Impossibly, even more than before, our eyes were glued to screens for hours upon end every day (and truthfully have never been fully peeled away) as we completed our homework, hung out with our friends, or even clocked in for work on Zoom. We re-binged our favorite TV shows and had countless movie marathons, online-shopped for hours with no access to a physical store, and played endless video games while just trying to feel something, I guess. While just a few weeks earlier we'd been lectured to by our parents to turn off our phones or computers, now we found ourselves in the unique situation of educating them on buying webcams and downloading software to continue going to work.

The social media apps we'd come to love just a few years earlier as a silly dumping ground for artsy pictures of our coffee or laughing at cat memes suddenly became a lifeline for any resemblance of human connection. Our online lives had finally become the "real" version of ourselves (which may have been the goal of these platforms all along) as we attempted to stay plugged into our normal lives in the midst of this "new normal" in any way we could.

Horrifyingly, the websites, apps, and platforms designed to keep us connected from afar started to make us feel more isolated and lonelier than ever before. We continued posting photos from the far-off "before," longing for a reason to wear anything other than sweatpants or go on a vacation again somewhere farther away than *another* walk around the block—but honestly, it just reminded us that the world would truly never be the happy-go-lucky, carefree place our parents told stories about from when they were our age. Too afraid to face the reality of what that might mean for our futures as adults, we quietly forced our smiles through missed proms and tossing our graduation caps over Zoom, through a screen.

Desperate to pass the time in what felt like a decade, we spent the next few years scrolling endlessly through TikTok trying to learn silly dances and find a reason to laugh again. Where we lacked connection with our peers was suddenly replaced by mega-influencers on a new viral app redefining internet culture—not with highly edited or curated photos of themselves or seemingly impossible lives, but with no-makeup videos getting ready in the morning or mini-vlogs cleaning their messy rooms. Forever changing the content we seek, TikTok became a window into the real human experience we all could relate to, instead of a glossy, filtered version of reality we could never quite identify with. To this day, our sense of wonder gravitating toward celebrities is no longer found in the too-perfect and unachievable, but instead, Gen Z has become desperately attracted to authenticity.

I guess in a world where everything is fake, edited, and put behind a screen, the most countercultural thing you can do is dare to be *real*.

Today in the 2020s as we've emerged from COVID, American life has never been more confusing. Political unrest has sparked violent protests (or "mostly peaceful," depending on which news outlets you follow). Health experts warn us about the dangers of COVID but fail to combat a growing mental health crisis taking the happiness and even lives of far too many in our generation. Everything—and I mean *Ev. Er. Y. Thing.*—from our education, our jobs, our entertainment, to our sexual intimacy experiences and dating lives, happens through a screen. Half of our states have outlawed abortion almost entirely, while others have actually legalized abortion in the "perinatal stage," opening a window to legalized infanticide. We've spent the last several years standing on the precipice of what experts tell us will likely become World War III, analyzing what might happen within our adult lives with Russia, China, or Iran. Singers create music videos giving lap dances to Satan, but you're canceled if you're an outspoken Christian in Hollywood. Half of America can't answer who we are trying to be as a nation; the other half wants to destroy the nation and rebuild it entirely. Pathetically, we can't even begin to answer the question "What is a woman?" More on all of that later.

It's hardly surprising, then, that a record low number of people say they are proud to be American.

In February 2023, the Morning Consult released a poll surveying generational attitudes about the United States. Their findings are staggering—while 73% of baby boomers report being proud to live in America, only 16% of Gen Zers do. The poll discovered that there has been a roughly 20 percentage point drop from generation to generation as our reality gets more and more complex and polarizing.[5]

When generations who came before us hear statistics like this, there's often a temptation to lash out at Gen Z—to blame us for "destroying" the foundation of America they love so much. Our predecessors say the reason we're not proud to live in this country is because the America we grew up in is so unrecognizable to them and what they were fortunate enough to love so much for decades. I can't tell you how often I've heard people say in political speeches or write in controversial social media posts: "Gen Z is destroying America." To those that regularly parrot this narrative or genuinely believe this sentiment, I challenge you to think critically about how a generation still in their teen and young adult years could have possibly destroyed the fabric of a nation that has stood the test of time from our very foundation. Was it Gen Z who flipped America upside down, or those who raised us? Educated us? Influenced us? Overmedicated and overdiagnosed us?

Is it possible to believe that my generation is hurting from our current state of affairs just as much as those who came before us—or maybe even more?

Broken Promises and Broken Hearts

As we've graduated from college and started planning for an unrecognizable future, again wading into uncharted waters for what our generation's story will become, we've faced other unprecedented obstacles. While those who came before us ordinarily would start thinking about settling down and starting a family, every aspect of our culture is telling us to abandon such dreams for ourselves.

Powerful politicians and celebrities urge us not to have children—why would we want to anyway, when it could be a detriment to the environment, is painful to our bodies to give birth, and ties us down with responsibility when we could work our way up a corporate ladder instead? We should honestly just get a puppy instead or become another increasingly popular "plant mom" we see on our social media feeds. We're told by our favorite movies and TV shows that marriage isn't a sacred institution bonding two people with God in an eternal covenant, but instead is a meaningless piece of paper that's really just good for a tax break. We're encouraged to date for as long as possible, with as many people as possible—after all, how will we know what we truly want in a long-term partner if we don't "try on" as many relationships as we can first? Besides, marriage is for boring *old* people. Who would genuinely want the fun and freedom of being young and crazy to stop?

What many have spent decades dismissing as fringe, out-there narratives eroding the foundations of committed love, marriage, and the family has quietly become the norm today for us Gen Zers entering our adult lives. The anything-goes, do-whatever-you-want, no-boundaries dating culture established for and normalized by millennials has eroded the traditional foundation of love so substantially that, heartbreakingly, Gen Z doesn't even want to participate in the first place.

I could tell you jarring statistics about the number of teenagers watching pornography every second in America—90% of boys and 60% of girls are exposed to pornography online before age 18, by the way.[6] I could blow your mind with the rising number of people embracing polyamory (dating multiple people at once rather than committing to just one) and the erosion of monogamous relationships from society. I could shock you with the horrifying number of people who have experienced sexual violence from the use of dating apps in the modern age (over 75% of dating app users in the last five years, according to one study).[7]

Truthfully, though, there's nothing as heartbreaking when it comes to Gen Z finding love than this—we're looking around at the state of affairs in how America conducts our most personal relationships; seeing the heartbreak, turmoil, and despair; and deciding *it's not even worth it* to risk the inevitable and devastating pain that we see most people encounter.

Pew Research recently found that a shocking 57% of single adults are not looking for a relationship—by casual dating or in a committed long-term partnership.[8] In a separate study, Pew Research found that 47% of American adults say dating has gotten culturally harder in the last ten years, and nearly 70% of poll respondents shared their dating lives were going "not too well" or "not at all well."[9]

How is it possible that in an anything-goes dating culture, where you're free to sleep with whomever you want, date as many people as possible, have "consequence-free" sex (which, truthfully, doesn't exist, though we like to pretend it does), and avoid "settling down," we've become miserable enough for a majority of single adults to avoid looking for love altogether? The falsehood of pornography has created unrealistic expectations of what intimacy is supposed to look like—and furthermore has encouraged us to seek intimacy through an artificial screen rather than building tangible intimacy with someone we love. Dating apps and rampant hookup culture have reinforced a societal norm rejecting long-term commitment and encouraging casual one-night stands instead of emotionally bonding with your best friend over decades in partnership. Polyamory has built a half-in, half-out culture of love that hinders us from giving our entire selves to our significant other, spreading ourselves far too thin to feel fulfilled.

With our love lives so bleak, it's easy to understand why we are living through the lowest marriage rate ever recorded in the United States since we even began recording marriage rates in 1867.[10] For those that do overcome the unlikelihood of getting married, prospects are bleak: nearly 50% of all marriages today end in divorce.[11] When the covenant of marriage and a promise "till death do us part" societally boils down to a piece of paper and a tax break, is it even surprising? And when we aren't putting ourselves out there, aren't falling in love, and aren't building marriages and forever relationships, we aren't building the foundations of family, either. In fact, the United States birth rate recently fell to its lowest level ever recorded—concerning enough to the point that we may not even be able to replace our current population![12]

Call me old-fashioned, but I believe Gen Z deserves to be whisked off our feet, to fall head-over-heels in love with the One, to have beautiful weddings and marriages and families. Sadly, as I write these words at 25 while wearing my engagement ring and preparing to marry my best friend, I have become an anomaly. No longer is falling in love, choosing commitment, and embarking on the journey of marriage the cultural "norm." Instead, I sometimes feel treated like an exotic zoo animal by my followers online who are shocked I met someone in *real life* (not on an app) and am actually committing the rest of my life to him. It breaks my heart to know that I am daydreaming about building a life and family and every day I fall more in love with my fiancé, while most in my generation can't even begin to wrap their heads around that lifestyle. America has systematically convinced itself that it was outdated, antiquated, and out-of-touch for the modern world, but has this narrative really just become a Trojan horse for more isolation and loneliness that my generation is already struggling with?

2024 America: The Upside Down

Today, it's inarguable that we live in the most advanced society in the world. The rise of political progressivism, technological innovation, commonality of higher education, and "enlightened" relationships makes it easy for us (at first blush) to believe that we are living in the best time in human history. After all, no generation before us could have ever dreamed of "having it all" the way we do, so it stands to reason that we should be the happiest and most joyful generation of all time. Right?

In case the picture I painted for you isn't clear enough throughout this chapter, the perfect, progressive, allegedly utopian society the last few generations have carefully built step-by-step has not translated to happiness, fulfillment, or even hope. Gen Z instead is facing the single greatest mental health crisis any generation has ever encountered in human history.

The world my generation has grown up and is coming into adulthood in has proved to be so at odds with human flourishing that we are setting records for mass anxiety, depression, substance abuse, and even suicide. The American Psychological Association reported in 2022 that 90% of my generation experienced physical or psychological symptoms as a result of stress within the prior year, and 70% of us report anxiety and depression to be major problems among our peers.[13] Furthermore, according to their findings, Gen Z adults are "more likely than some other generations to report they have been diagnosed with an anxiety disorder (18%) and more likely than all other generations to report they have been diagnosed with depression (23%)."

The National Institute on Drug Abuse is raising concerns about our higher likelihood to develop addiction, reporting that nearly 25% of twelfth graders used illicit drugs in 2015 (the year I graduated from high school).[14] The National Institute on Alcohol Abuse and Alcoholism recently found more than 4.2 million people between the ages of 12 and 20 confessed to binge-drinking. TWELVE. YEARS. OLD.[15]

Most recently (and most devastatingly), the CDC shared new data in early 2023 finding teen girls are facing record levels of hopelessness and persistent sadness—so much so that one in three teenage girls in America seriously considered suicide in 2021. *One* in *three*. In that same year, 13% of teenage girls actually attempted to take their own life. Those who didn't act on their feelings aren't doing much better, either—three in five teenage girls felt persistently sad and hopeless, a figure that increased 60% from a decade earlier.[16] Influencers, politicians, and celebrities continue echoing the shallow narrative that we "aren't alone," but no one in any substantial position of power seems to want to acknowledge just how much we're struggling, let alone begin creating meaningful solutions.

That perfect future world our grandparents and parents so carefully built, where we'd inevitably have flying cars and world peace, really looks a lot more dystopian than anyone ever expected it would. With the exception of George Orwell, I suppose, who I am still convinced is a time traveler, it often feels like no one could have seen this chapter of history coming—2024 America feels eerily similar to an Orwellian *1984*, hallmarked by censorship, authoritarianism, and indoctrination. The same inversion of reality where truth is propaganda, love is war, and groupthink is freedom has come for modern America—and we barely even noticed it quietly taking hold of our society over the last several decades.

As those with quiet positions of power have played the long game over the past several decades, slowly changing the fabric of American culture as we know it through every pillar of our society, we've suddenly "woken up" in the 2020s flabbergasted as to how we got here and looking for someone to blame.

It's so much easier to point the finger at Gen Z for the source of today's problems. After all, it's painful to look in the mirror and admit complacency—that your wildest dreams for how bad society could become would eventually come true because you, and America at large, simply weren't paying attention. Sadly, though, as we've slowly watched our schools, entertainment, media, politics, churches, and corporations transform into vehicles for the Left's authoritarian agenda, it's been Gen Z who has had to pay the price...and it's Gen Z who will be left to clean up the mess after everyone else is gone.

When I give speeches about the unique cultural identity of my generation to political fundraisers, conferences, and large events across America, I always like to start with the foundational concepts of this very chapter. I often hear baby boomers and Gen Xers say, "Well, when I was that age, I dealt with stress. I figured it out. I got through it. Once these kids grow up and enter the 'real world,' they'll get it." In a chapter of history where the "real world" did mean hoisting yourself up by your bootstraps and "figuring it out," come hell or high water, I'm sure that sentiment was helpful for young people seeking meaning and a purpose-driven path forward. Today, though, everything you've read in this chapter *is* the "real world" for Gen Z.

In 2024 America, our day-to-day life could not be more fundamentally juxtaposed to anything our parents experienced at our same age. The easiest way to explain it is to borrow a phrase from one of my favorite TV shows of all time, *Stranger Things*: we are quite literally living in the upside down, in an inverted reality from what should be recognizable and familiar. Right is wrong and wrong is right. Men are women and women are men. Those who disagree with us aren't just different—they're evil. We're rewriting history to fit today's political agendas, giving no thought to how that will impact the future. Sexual liberation pushing us to sleep with whoever we want has resulted in people not seeking out relationships at all. It's become considered morally superior to expose children to adult sexual conversations in elementary school than to shield them and protect their innocence. In fact, you're a "better person" today if you tell a struggling 12-year-old to undergo genital mutilation surgery and hormone "therapy" rather than to seek mental health treatment if she suddenly comes home with no history of gender dysphoria and says she no longer wants to be a girl (which, let's face it, if one in three of them are genuinely considering suicide, who *would* want to be one?). Rather than building the future Martin Luther King Jr. so eloquently dreamed of, where we'd be judged by the content of our character instead of the color of our skin, we're segregating our dorm rooms and implementing the debunked *1619 Project* curriculum claiming the basis of America's foundation was slavery. For goodness' sake, our new food pyramid literally tells us that Lucky Charms marshmallows are healthier than steak.[17]

In 2024 America, nothing is authentic. We truly live in an artificial reality, where my generation has no way to parse through the noise and chaos to even determine truth to begin with. We've spent the past several years hiding—hiding our smiles behind masks, hiding our eyes behind VR headsets, and hiding our lives behind screens and social media profiles.

In 2024 America, it's time to break free of the spiral into insanity we've been wrapped up in throughout our entire generational lifetime. Gen Z is nostalgic for a time we don't even remember and weren't ever (or at the very least, barely) around for. Our fashion trends, music choices, and favorite television shows scream decades past as we attempt to resurrect any semblance of a chapter in American history where people could exist without all hell breaking loose. We recycle clothing trends from every decade, from bell-bottom jeans to Crocs and everything in between, sometimes all at the same time. We blare music from our parents' young adult years (conveniently also the soundtrack hits to modern-day *Guardians of the Galaxy*), savoring the simplicity of a real guitar and clean vocals. We binge *Friends* and *The Office* over and over again, wishing we could have friends we actually spent time with out from behind a screen or laugh with our coworkers in the break room rather than be forced to work through Zoom.

Through every passing moment, Gen Z is desperately longing for a return to reality. It may not look like the early twenties of our grandparents and parents, but we're taking back the cultural driver's seat to build our own American dream. It goes without saying from what you've read in these past few pages that we are different, given our upbringing—so, as we grow into adulthood in the upside down, who are we *really*?

punk rock patriots

If you'd have told me on my first day as a Biomedical Sciences major in college that I'd eventually spend a significant portion of my career working in politics, I'd have looked at you like you had three heads. I came to work in politics in a roundabout way, never planning on making something that was no more than a hobby part of my professional journey and career. While being raised by two Catholic lawyers for parents certainly piqued my interest in a good debate and our system of governance, my plan was always to work in medicine (all the way through college!). Wearing suits in my early twenties and working for the United States Senate and even the White House was *never* on my radar, but there I found myself smack dab in the middle of "how the sausage is made"—as we often described Washington—during two internships in college. I also worked for several political nonprofits and appeared on national television advocating for political issues as a Gen Z voice following graduate school.

It came as a complete surprise, then, while working at the White House during the 2018 summer internship class, when my mom shared a sweet story with me: Many, many years before, my kindergarten teacher had told my parents during parent-teacher conferences that she predicted someday I would become president of the United States. It seemed I loved to "provide direction" to my classmates (probably a nice way of saying I was a little bossy...I was the oldest of three headstrong girls—can you blame me?) and had natural leadership skills. The sentiment was so kind and brought a huge smile to my face at 21 years old—who would have thought that same little girl who never dreamed of working in politics would somehow end up working in the White House?

Politics, medicine, or anything else I set my mind to was always encouraged as an obtainable reality in my home growing up. My siblings and I were pushed by our parents to reach for the stars and dream big, knowing there was nothing we couldn't accomplish if we were willing to put the work in. If I close my eyes, I can still hear my dad repeat his favorite inspirational mantra: "Hard work beats talent when talent doesn't work hard." It didn't matter if we were inherently the smartest, most creative, or had the most resources. Simply having the opportunity to live in a modern, free America was the only foundation we needed to build our own American Dream. My parents loved sharing their stories of growing up as the youngest of five and six kids, respectively, paying their own way through college and law school, overcoming financial and cultural barriers to turn their dreams into a reality. I can't tell you how many times I was told the story of my mom arriving for her first day of college at 17 in the '80s with $250 cash and an old beater Volkswagen, forced to figure it out if she wanted to accomplish more with her life than her high school classmates in Post Falls, Idaho, who were working odd jobs or were already in prison. Mom and Dad loved to remind us girls that, comparatively, we had it easy, and we agreed. After all, we were growing up in a new millennium with a constantly changing world—if there was ever a time to turn your dreams into a reality, it was going to happen in the 2000s.

The same sentiment was often echoed throughout the formative years of other Gen Zers. We started being asked in preschool what we dreamed of doing when we grew up, and we were encouraged to pursue anything our heart longed for. If I remember correctly, my love of dogs made my first answer in preschool a "pet store owner," which evolved into "veterinarian" and eventually "doctor" by the time I started high school. Common answers from my peers included "astronaut," "actress," "surgeon," or even "president of the United States." The crazy thing was—any of that could be true! In an era consistently defined by innovation and change, truly anything could become our reality if we were willing to make it happen. Especially in the "hope and change" era of Barack Obama's 2008 presidential campaign, it seemed everyone around us shared the belief that your future could be anything you wanted if you were daring to dream big enough, regardless of your political affiliation. As we now know, the cultural impact of this election would shape politics forevermore, taking us from the stiff and rehearsed presidents of generations past to punchy, unique leaders with the capacity to change American culture as a whole—instead of merely advocating tax policy or legislation. *Thanks, Obama.* Actually, though.

All of a sudden, *hope* became a mantra regularly repeated for my generation—and it stuck. Call it propaganda, too-powerful media narratives, or naïveté, but it felt pretty damn good to have something to cling to as a child observing your concerned parents regularly reflect on a rapidly changing reality.

Watching the world transform before our very eyes sparked a wonder and natural curiosity within our hearts that we desperately longed to be a part of. A changing world meant an opportunity to make your mark and leave a legacy, and Gen Z knew from an early age that our role in this evolution would be vitally important. Naturally, then, it goes without saying that we are a generation of dreamers. We believe anything is possible and want to challenge the status quo, particularly because our status quo has quickly transformed from a world of whimsy and joy to a dystopian future of authoritarianism, too-powerful technology run amok, and social anarchy threatening to destroy the fabric of our nation as we know it.

We're willing to fight for a better world and a stronger future for those who come after us, and we have no problem challenging authority if that's what it takes to get there. We're young, but we believe our youth is a strength rather than a weakness and provides a unique vantage point from which to change culture for the better. In many ways, that's been interpreted by those who came before us as defiant, whiny, youthful ignorance—but our outlook and drive stem from our wealth of experiences from living in a broken reality. We know all too intimately what happens in a world where you *can* do anything, but perhaps *shouldn't*. After all, we can 3D-print human organs, but in a world where one in three teenage girls are genuinely contemplating taking their own life due to chronic depression and hopelessness, what good is a spare organ?

That's not to say we're perpetually on the same page or in agreement. Rather, Gen Z is a powerfully unique cohort down to each individual. Growing up in a world where we were told we can be, do, and accomplish anything has turned the key and unlocked limitless opportunities to craft our own identities. That being said, the tough thing about this book is I can never begin to attempt to provide a "one-size-fits-all" definition of who my generation is and who we will become. There is no box we could perfectly fit inside, which clearly shines through in our fierce independence. We're rejecting the prescribed pathways to success and happiness those who came before us demanded, opting for entrepreneurship and innovation over today's often meaningless four-year degrees. We're throwing in the towel on the two-party political system, instead gravitating toward independence from the political machine. We're moving away from hookup culture and meaningless sex, deciding for ourselves that culture's boundaries have gone too far. We're embracing activism with our purchasing power and aligning with companies that share our values, even at such a young age. More on all of that later.

We often disagree on the most pressing social issues of our day. We have overwhelmingly different religious perspectives and cultural influences. We are coming into adulthood in an increasingly divided and complicated reality, where no one can quite predict where we go from here. Truly, our world has never been as confusing, frustrating, and unstable as it is now. Despite our culture's instability, though, Gen Z remains hopeful and idealistic as a whole. In fact, Wunderman Thompson Data tells us that 75% of my generation believes we *will* change the world. Pause. Whoa—read that again. SEVENTY-FIVE percent.[1]

That's a pretty universal belief for a single generation—and is particularly impressive when you consider Gen Z's unique position as America's most diverse nation in history when it comes to race, ethnicity, and sexual orientation.[2] Where our increasingly divisive culture continues to attempt to separate us on the basis of our race, our gender identity, our political affiliation, and more, we remain united in the simple belief that we have the capacity and the willingness to change the world for the better. When I first discovered that statistic, I was floored. In the midst of unprecedented division and hatred for those different from ourselves in America, we are locking arms together, willing to fight for a return to reality and a stronger future for all of us. Drowning out the noise of politicians, media talking heads, and celebrities who seek to tear us apart, we remain steadfast in our mission to change the world for the better.

And here's the best part of it all—we aren't waiting for permission or "our turn" to make an impact.

A Country for Old White Men?

I often speak to groups on high school and college campuses about the future of America and where we go from here. In order to even remotely provide direction into the future, I always believe it's important to visit the past, so one of my favorite conversations I love to have on campus is asking students to "describe what the Founding Fathers looked like." There's typically a litany of familiar responses, from simply "old" to "wrinkly, ancient white men." The comical descriptions paint a picture of sagging, geriatric, half-dead figures who couldn't possibly be in tune with culture, right?

The "old white men" mantra of those who shaped our country has been repeated over and over again so often that an entire generation has been conditioned to believe it unequivocally. We're told that our founding documents couldn't possibly stand the test of time or relate to us today, because they probably didn't even relate to the earliest Americans! How could they, when they were written by people completely out of touch? This line of thinking is used as a Trojan horse to destroy the very foundations of Western civilization, including the freedom and sense of subjective morality based in Judeo-Christian values that has transformed humanity for the better—all while convincing kids and young adults they essentially grew up in *The Princess Bride*'s pit of despair instead of the freest country the world has ever known.

I believed the "old white men" story for many years myself, likely pulling memories from illustrations in my AP United States History textbooks or historic paintings I'd seen of our nation's Founders. How short our memories are, misleading us on our own history.

The bold men and women of the eighteenth century who changed the course of human history with the founding of the United States of America were not on their way to a well-earned grave. Rather, they led the battle for freedom from within the heartbeat of culture in their teenage and young adult years, fighting for a future rooted in liberty for those who would come after them. On July 4, 1776, James Monroe was only 18 years old. Aaron Burr and John Marshall were only 20 years old. Before becoming the star of a smash-hit Broadway musical, Alexander Hamilton was only 21 years old. Betsy Ross was 24, James Madison was 25, and Thomas Jefferson was only 33 years old on the day we declared independence from authoritarianism. Our first president, consistently depicted as the oldest of the group with sagging eyes and white, thinning hair, was only 44 years old.[3]

It turns out, the average age of the signatories to the Declaration of Independence was 44 years old, and *more than a dozen* were under the age of 35 (easily the most impactful names we still refer to today). Contrast that with the unbelievably old age of the most powerful people in America today—a Congress housing seemingly countless 70- to 90-year-olds and an executive branch with more of the same. In 2020, we elected the oldest president in United States history, inaugurated at 78 years old. In 2021, the *Washington Post* reported on the oldest Senate in American history, asking the question, "How old is too old to be a United States senator?" Senator Dianne Feinstein, a Democrat from California, held public office for 32 years and was 90 years old, requiring significant assistance from her staff, before she actually *died* of old age in office last year. Senator Chuck Grassley, a Republican from Iowa, is just a few months younger and has held his Senate seat representing Iowa *since 1981* (fun fact, that's sixteen years before I was even born).[4]

We've transitioned from a young, rebellious national leadership to a rapidly aging and culturally out-of-touch one within just a few generations, and yet we are consistently told by those in power we need to wait until we have enough "life experience" to take on a leadership role to craft a stronger future. I'm not sure who needs to hear these words today, but I am here to tell you in no uncertain terms: That. Is. A. Lie.

You do not need to be past the retirement age to run for office. You don't need to have been with a single company for decades to obtain business experience. You don't need to be married or a parent to care about the next generation after you. You don't need to work for years in broadcast journalism to start sharing your opinions publicly. You don't need to "wait your turn" for those in power to decide they're tired of Capitol Hill (or, frankly, to die) to run for office.

In truth, America has always relied on young, punk rock patriots standing for freedom against older generations in power, even before we were formally a nation. We were *never* designed to be a "sit down, shut up, and wait your turn" nation, and Gen Z knows it's high time we return to our roots. We aren't waiting for permission to speak up or to lead. Instead, we're taking advantage of our youth to stand up in innovative and exciting ways.

Every January, tens of thousands of teenagers and young adults descend on Washington, DC, for the annual March for Life, branding ourselves the "Pro-Life Generation" and demanding our most basic human right—the right to life—for everyone who comes after us. Having attended several years in a row myself, it's a deeply powerful, vibrant, and youthful experience. When I first showed up to the National Mall for my first March for Life in January 2020 while living in Washington, I expected a crowd of middle-aged middle Americans—you know, the type you'd expect to talk about abortion on the news but have little personal experience with the issue. Instead, I found myself surrounded by tens of thousands of high schoolers and college students who'd traveled in buses, on trains, and by flying to descend on the steps of the Supreme Court on a freezing Saturday morning. This was no movement of "old white men," but of a diverse tapestry of young voices demanding cultural and political change for our generation.

Countless other teens have descended on Washington for the March for Our Lives, organized by survivors of the high school shooting in Parkland, to demand school safety and gun control. Others protest nationwide to call attention to environmental disasters impacting our public lands. Agree or disagree with any event, you can't for a moment begin to deny the power of youth activism being reshaped every day.

Youth organizations founded by teenagers and twenty-somethings are fostering debates and dialogue on college campuses that university administrators are failing to facilitate—from Turning Point USA and Students for Life to the Young Democratic Socialists of America.

Rejecting the stiff and formal deliverance of news by traditional media, we're engaging with independent journalism and informal social media content to understand the world around us. In fact, the American Press Institute has found that an overwhelming 74% of Gen Zers consume daily news through social media.[5] We watch livestreams facilitated by twenty-somethings wearing sweatpants in the spare bedroom of their apartments instead of fancy news broadcasts with talking heads wearing suits. We scroll through TikTok or Instagram for hours on end to understand what's happening in the world and how we should feel about it. YouTube has become our hub for commentary, and we trust it far more than CNN or MSNBC.

Every moment of every day, we have access to all the information in the history of the universe. It's insane to even attempt to wrap your mind around, but it's shaping how we think and feel about our culture with each passing second. After all, given the choice between curiosity and ignorance, between infinite information and complete oblivion—which decision would anyone make?

While our parents practically spent their teen and young adult years caring about anything *but* politics, we are engaging with politically charged content constantly. We're watching viral videos of the president of the United States or commenting on hotly contested social media debates covering abortion, climate, gender identity, and more. We're sharing controversial opinions and seeking answers to the big cultural questions far earlier than most older generations give us credit for under the assumption that we couldn't possibly care about politics or social issues at a young age. In reality, however, Gen Z understands a fundamental truth: we don't have the luxury of sitting on the sidelines in an increasingly complicated world. America desperately needs leadership now, a challenge we are ready to rise to the occasion for.

I couldn't even begin to tell you how often I scroll through social media and come across sentiments like "Gen Z hates America," or "Gen Z couldn't care less about politics." The problem with their philosophy is simple: we *do* care. A lot. While many who came before us assume we won't even be ready to think about the economy, environmental policy, abortion, taxes, etc., we've already taken the time to make up our minds on each subject.

The political Left understands this far more than the Right and has capitalized on it, encouraging kids at any age to get involved in culture and politics alike. They've successfully generated a branding and marketing strategy to convince an entire generation that the only way to build a stronger future is to align with left-wing policies and causes—after all, if conservatives don't even have the awareness to communicate with you as a young person, how could their policies possibly make your life better?

For many decades, there's been a long-running joke that if you aren't a liberal in America when you're 20, then you have no heart. But if you aren't a conservative by the time you're 50, then you have no brain. It's a sentiment to chuckle at, at the very least, but it has driven the Right's strategy of approaching youth for far too long. Conservatives assume that it's a done deal for teenagers and twenty-somethings to embrace overwhelmingly left-wing policies and feel-good politics, but by the time they enter the "real world" and face the crushing burden of taxes, home ownership, raising children, and corporate America, they'll change their minds. One can only embrace happy-go-lucky idealism for so long, right?

Wrong. So wrong. In reality, as you know from this book, the "real world" has fundamentally transformed into something unrecognizable compared to when our parents were our age. Up is down. Down is up. Right is wrong. Wrong is right. Men are women. Women are men... In the words of President Joe Biden, you know the thing.

Moreover, the *Financial Times* has closely studied voting patterns of millennials in the United States and United Kingdom, finding they're "shattering the oldest rule in politics"—unlike the silent generation, boomers, and Gen X, they're trending more left-wing as they age.[6] It's easy to assume we will follow suit.

Gen Z has been systematically targeted by a single narrative for most of our childhood, adolescence, and young adult years to embrace collectivism, moral relativism, and even socialism—all while those claiming to conserve traditional values into the future refuse to have a conversation with the next generation to begin with. It's no wonder, then, that we have leaned so heavily into the feelings-based politics tugging at our heartstrings instead of sometimes seeing the bigger picture, much to the despair and confusion of conservative leaders.

Facts versus Feelings

A popular mantra coined by conservative commentator and author Ben Shapiro began picking up steam toward the end of my high school years—"facts don't care about your feelings." In other words, your feelings on an issue don't change reality or objective truth, irrespective of how strongly you feel or what emotions that issue invokes. It's true, beyond a shadow of a doubt, and ironically often makes people upset to hear.

The "facts don't care about your feelings" sentiment worked unbelievably well in marketing conservative ideas to millennials—who, frankly, sometimes needed a verbal roundhouse kick to the face with objective truth. This mantra was arguably single-handedly responsible for the rise of Ben Shapiro and his organization, the Daily Wire, which today has amassed a following of millions upon millions worldwide and given a platform to star-power social commentators like Michael Knowles and Brett Cooper. It stirred debates on college campuses and fiery arguments in social media comments sections and even made appearances in speeches by prominent politicians.

It's a powerful, simple sentiment that has "red-pilled" countless people across America (and the world!) to reject our culture's push toward subjective truth and moral relativism, but I've seen it taken so far that many right-of-center content creators, commentators, and political voices have suggested feelings are something to be avoided at all costs. After all, if it wasn't for manipulation of feelings, these people often say, we wouldn't have arrived in a time where there are an unlimited number of genders or "shout your abortion" campaigns. It's got to be cold, hard facts, or nothing.

The problem today, though, is that Gen Z is a "feelings" generation. We were raised and educated to consistently be mindful of our feelings and those of others in a "self-care" culture. Our school curriculum often involved aspects of social-emotional learning, or SEL, where we were instructed to view the world through a lens of empathy. When we are passionate about something, we channel our strongest emotions to drive our behavior, taking to the streets to protest injustices or igniting social activism campaigns online. We care about the world around us, politically, socially, and culturally, because we *feel* so strongly about making a difference.

Feelings can be, and certainly have been, manipulated to push a political agenda. We've seen the playbook roll out before our eyes—changing societal definitions of gender, facilitating the removal of Judeo-Christian values from Western society, and even attempting to destroy the nuclear family. But in reality, feelings are an inherent aspect of the human experience. While they can be a vehicle for damage and destruction, they can also be a vehicle for good.

I often share with my peers, if you *really care* about women, you should fight for an end to abortion—so women's lives are no longer at risk (not to mention millions of lost children) and our society doesn't push you into a corner choosing between a career and a family. If you *really care* about ending poverty, you should fight for free markets and genuine capitalism (not so much the big government-big corporation version we have now), because no other economic system in history has lifted this many people out of financial ruin and into security for their future. If you *really care* about environmental conservation, you should fight for hunting, fishing, ranching, and farming—after all, no one else has nearly as much of a vested interest in the health of the environment. If you *really care* about affordable health care for all, you should be fighting for more competition and greater price transparency, not greater government control.

Of course, there is absolutely a time and place for facts trumping feelings—our feelings are fleeting, while the truth is steadfast. Arguably, no one has been in greater need of a sense of objective reality than Gen Z, who has been raised to believe even truth is subjective from person-to-person. Facts, rooted in truth, will always be something to rely on when fighting the whims of often fallible and misleading feelings of humanity—but facts and feelings can work hand in hand to communicate truth far more effectively than in isolation.

Incredibly, even with a right-of-center vexation with the "feelings generation" and a left-of-center dominance on youth messaging, we have jolted the American political system by rejecting partisanship, period. Recent Gallup polling has discovered 52% of Gen Zers are sticking with a politically "Independent" label, while only 17% of us identify as Republicans and 31% as Democrats.[7]

On the issues, it's easy to assume the overwhelming left-wing narrative that has pervaded our education, entertainment, church sermons, and social media feeds have driven our opinions. Shockingly, as the oldest of us began to vote in the controversial 2016 presidential election cycle, national polling found Gen Z to be the most conservative generation on an issue-by-issue basis since World War II. In a 2017 article entitled "Why Democrats Should Be Losing Sleep Over Generation Z," *Forbes* magazine made the case for Gen Z as more individualistic, more conservative both fiscally and socially, and making greater waves of impact in our political system than our millennial predecessors.[8]

In 2022, we turned out in huge numbers to vote our values, contrary to anyone's expectations: 27% of 18- to 29-year-olds turned out to vote in the last midterm election—the second-highest youth voter turnout in history.[9] Despite leaning left, Democrats lost significant support with youth voters compared to the last midterm election in 2018, -7 points for 18- to

29-year-olds.[10] Gearing up for this year's presidential election, it's anyone's guess where Gen Z's loyalties will lie. One thing is clear: it's hard to win us over, and we refuse to blindly support those in power without asking the tough questions and making up our own minds first.

As our country becomes increasingly divided, complicated, and upside down, America's next great generation is hungry for answers to the big questions in culture. We're ready to break free from prescribed narratives and shallow talking points, shattering the institutions relying on assumed youthful ignorance. As a generation of dreamers, we continue to idealize what culture will become, and we're willing to fight like hell to turn our American Dreams into reality. While many cower in fear attempting to answer where we go from here, we are a generation made for such a time as this, boldly embracing the call to lead our culture into a stronger future.

Not that it even needs to be said, but it's time for Gen Z to take back the reins. Older generations may be those in power today, but the future belongs to us, and it's up to each of us to take a seat at the table in conserving freedom for those to come. Together, we're prioritizing individual liberty, and where we truly stand on the issues just may shock you.

CHAPTER 4

beyond the echo chamber

"Gen Z is so confused. WTF."

"Give me one good reason why eighteen-year-olds should be allowed to vote. I can't think of ANY."

"Gen Z is the most illogical generation in our nation's history."

"Y'all Gen Z'ers will destroy America."

One of my favorite pastimes in the last few election cycles has become scrolling through Twitter and confronting the overwhelming generational bias against teenagers and young adults. Despite seemingly countless evidence to the contrary, it seems like every day I confront content blaming Gen Z for all of America's problems, largely from people who politically agree with me and work to "change hearts and minds" as right-of-center content creators!

We are labeled stupid, uneducated, lazy, entitled, spoiled, and all-around maleficent by many who refuse to even ask *why* we believe the things we do (let alone seek to understand). We've been written off as a generation before we've even had the chance to write our own chapter of history. After the 2022 midterm elections, we were assumed to be an entire generation of leftist activists hell-bent on destroying the very fabric of our nation's tradition and history. Why? Because we voted the majority of the time with Democrats—but those labeling us as such failed to take into account our significant trajectory of voting *more conservatively* as a generation compared to 2018 and 2020!

The truth about our political identity is not as simple as a blue or red bumper sticker on our cars or a party letter affiliation next to our name. We're more skeptical than our millennial predecessors about media, traditional institutions, and even the companies we financially support.[1] When surveyed about personal values, 92% of us report authenticity to be more important than anything else—more than getting rich or famous, spending time on things that will help our futures, or even changing the world, according to EY.[2] We aren't interested in an edited or overmarketed version of the products we buy, the media we consume, or the policies we're told to support. Rather, if something is too "marketed," we'll scroll right past as fast as we can.

Our natural skepticism and gravitation toward authenticity may be why we're distancing ourselves from the rigidity of the two-party political system and opting for independence in staggering numbers (with 52% of us identifying as Independent over Republican/Democrat, according to a Gallup poll from 2022).[3] Gen Z's remarkable political independence has created unique circumstances for generational opinions on specific political issues. We realize that we are living in perhaps the most divided time in modern history, not so much because of the perceived Right versus Left tug-of-war, but because of a generational chasm which has led us to live in two different Americas in the 2020s. Our sense of reality is fundamentally juxtaposed with that of our parents and grandparents as we grow up in the upside down, so it stands to reason that our political perspectives will be different as well.

While overwhelming left-wing bias has permeated our cultural experiences through education, entertainment, religious institutions, social media, traditional media, and of course, politics, it's worth exploring how that bias has been allowed to thrive. We do have a left-of-center lean as a generation—and it shows, so far, at the ballot box—but that's not because we're hell-bent on destroying traditional American values or even that we aren't interested in another viewpoint. It's simply all that we're ever exposed to, and we are rarely given the opportunity to challenge our own perspectives with opposing voices. Social media feeds, our classrooms, and even our workplaces have become echo chambers of people who think, speak, and act exactly the same way.

Beyond the astounding left-wing bias that has permeated academia that I've told you about, perhaps the biggest contributor to Gen Z's echo chambers is the ambiguous digital algorithms controlling what we see and who we interact with in the digital space we spend the vast majority of our time immersed in. Multimedia website Big Think explains social media algorithms as something that can easily "manipulate" you. In an October 2017 article, they say algorithms allow information to be transmitted via "complex contagion," and that "social media platforms rely heavily on people's behavior to decide on the content that you see. In particular, they watch for content that people respond to or 'engage' with by liking, commenting and sharing."[4]

In other words, the content you typically would gravitate toward or generally agree with driving you to engage with a post or video continues to be amplified in your feed over and over again. Suddenly, commenting "Couldn't agree more!" on a post about third-wave feminism causes your feed to be flooded with content from the annual Women's March, Planned Parenthood, and accounts dedicated to amplifying the feminist message. Throughout the week, month, and year, the cycle continues with more content pushing you further into an echo chamber. Rinse and repeat.

Not only are we consistently encouraged by the algorithm to consume content we generally agree with, but we're further driven to *create* it. Scientists have studied the brain's response to social media's overwhelming variety of stimuli (such as likes, comments, DMs, etc.) keeping us perpetually glued to our screens—and it turns out there's a reason they call us social media *users*. The same neurological pathways responsible for driving human behavior to seek food, shelter, and a sexual mate through the release of dopamine are also closely linked to addiction. When an addict gets a "high," the rush is linked to a release of dopamine from the brain, making us feel pleasure and satisfaction and a desire to repeat the process. Today, though, a smartphone and social media app have become just as much a vehicle for addiction and that same dopamine release as a hypodermic needle.

Resident psychiatrist at Stanford and director of clinical innovation at Stanford Brainstorm Dr. Sara Johansen says social media has the potential to be a powerful addiction in anyone's life. When your phone lights up with a notification that someone "liked" your photo, the exact same dopamine pathways linked to motivation to survive, reward for success, and addiction are energized. Dr. Johansen explains we become hooked on social media like a drug not just due to the "pleasure of the like" but further the "intermittent absence of the like."[5]

Simply put, we're motivated to seek engagement with the content we create—be it a photo from your most recent family vacation or a meme poking fun at the president's latest blunder—and what better way to receive a flood of engagement than creating content that you know will resonate well with the people you politically agree with and see consistently on your own feed? From the consumer perspective to the creator side, social media has created the very definition of an echo chamber for each and every one of us, amplifying content to us that we'll likely engage with and be energized by and rewarding us when we create content that will do the same for others.

Our dissemination of information, therefore, has become entirely opinionated. There truly is no such thing as an "unbiased" source of information when we consume the vast majority of our news, current events, and commentary through a social media platform that is determined to push an agenda (one way or another) to each of its users in a highly curated and personally tailored way. The same model has been replicated off-screen, in our friend groups, work colleagues, college classes, and more. Algorithms have, whether we've realized it or not, essentially trained our brains to solely seek out information we are inclined to agree with and respond to positively, instead of engaging in dialogue that will challenge our perspectives.

When the majority of Gen Z's echo chambers on- and offscreen have encapsulated a partisan identity, it's no wonder we as a generation have embraced, at the least, a lean to the left. When we are constantly surrounded by the beating drum of only one side of the conversation, it's difficult to hear the faint tune of another perspective playing in the distance. Although the label America has decided to slap on our generation at large for being a bunch of whiny, entitled socialists is not true, it's believed and amplified by many who came before us. As a result, conservatives in particular are often outraged by our political opinions (even when we have a notably *conservative* trajectory in our voting behavior and stances at the issue-by-issue level), and the "Gen Z is a lost cause" Twitter gang continues furiously typing, day after day.

Don't get me wrong—many on the political Left chastise Gen Z the same way. Our vice president, Kamala Harris, recently went viral for a resurfaced 2015 clip in which she said, "What else do we know about this population, 18 through 24? They are stupid. That is why we put them in dormitories. And they have a resident assistant. They make really bad decisions."[6] *Stupid.* Seems like an odd word to choose when you're also trying to rally and encourage young people to get involved in politics.

More often than not, though, it *is* the political Left who intentionally and boldly champions our generation for our role as the future of American culture. For better or worse, and perhaps without even consciously realizing it for ourselves, we've embraced another set of echo chambers in politics. We've subconsciously embraced the supposed "truth" that the Left is the side of youth, progress, and the future, while the Right must chastise young people for their "ignorance" in believing left-wing viewpoints—even when it's to our own demise.

As a result, far too many older conservatives condemn, castigate, and isolate themselves from Gen Z by suggesting that we must be "stupid" for not embracing conservative values—when we have rarely even been given the opportunity to be acquainted with them in the first place. How could we, when our education system, entertainment industry, social media feeds, and even many of our churches have become amplifiers for the echo chamber of modern cultural leftism? When one half of the American political spectrum takes the time to educate the next generation and uplift us with words of encouragement, while the other often ostracizes us and labels us "uneducated," how do you think we're going to lean?

Incredibly, and to the surprise of many who may be reading these words today, Gen Z is *not* the socialist, authoritarian, Marxist generation too many conservatives assume we are and too many leftists dream we would be. We're breaking the political echo chamber of Right versus Left, Republican versus Democrat, conservative versus liberal, capitalist versus socialist. The "your generation is a lost cause" talking point I confront every day in Instagram comments and quote Tweets could not be further from the truth. We are answering the call to lead, transcending the political barriers that far too often divide our society and are instead rebuilding a truly *United* States of America dedicated to improving the lives of those who come after us. There is no reason to have anything but hope for one another and our generation as we continue to grow into adulthood and seek opportunities for leadership.

If you're outspoken about your values like me, you may have brushed up against the misplaced, manufactured "Gen Z is destroying America" outrage from your parents or grandparents, teachers, or family friends. There's a powerful misinformation campaign spreading among America's political Right about our generational identity and the important role we must play in fighting for a stronger future. Alongside this misinformation has grown a manipulative political Left claiming to uplift and empower young voices, eager to include us in their movement without truly explaining what legacy their policies will leave us: empty, broken, poor, and lost.

I believe most of Gen Z's supposed "ignorant" reputation truly comes from our status as a "feelings generation," knowing we are primarily motivated by empathy for others rather than the hard, logical facts of those who came before us. As I've already covered, feelings can be a powerful tool to manipulate a demographic while pushing a political agenda, and they are more often than not utilized by the Left rather than the Right in American politics. Therefore, Gen Z's seemingly unified embrace of abortion, gender theory, critical race theory, and more has been driven by a twisted narrative telling us if we care about women, our peers struggling with their identity, and ending racism—the only way to manifest our empathy is through a leftist approach. Sadly, this superficial approach fails to tell us the whole truth:

this very approach will only facilitate more chaos, confusion, anger, and division—not to mention brokenness—as we lean further into it.

If we *actually* cared about women, we wouldn't be promoting an industry dedicated to ending the life of her innocent preborn child and putting her life at risk, causing irreparable psychological damage along the way. If we *actually* cared about racism, we wouldn't be amplifying the message of segregation our nation fought so long to abolish in our Ivy League dorm rooms and college graduation ceremonies. If we *actually* cared about our friends struggling with their identities, we wouldn't encourage them to irreversibly chemically or surgically castrate themselves before they've even finished going through puberty...you get the picture.

These are easy issues to win on—it's difficult to argue with reality—but until we're willing to fight on offense for the truth, we'll have to settle with the shallow facade of empathy presented by the Left. Once we are willing to fight, I believe that conservatives' willingness to embrace Gen Z with open arms for real conversation about solutions to the problems our society faces will be a dramatic turning point for the future of American politics and culture alike. We just have to be willing to have that conversation in the first place.

If we are to have any hope for a return to rationalism, respect for one another, and reality as we know it, Gen Z can no longer be isolated from or cast aside by those who came before us. It's time for true dialogue to return to the American experience, across the political aisle and the generational divide. We as a generation are naturally curious, hungry for a change of perspective, and yearning for a depth of discourse that goes beyond 280 characters on a screen—but without exposure to conservative ideas in an increasingly leftist world, we'll never be able to.

In this chapter, as we dive deeper into what we believe as a generation and where we have room to change our perspectives, it should go without saying that the next few pages couldn't possibly be indicative of the opinions of an *entire* generation. We're talking about a generation of nearly 70 million people (if you're a math person, you can calculate that to be about 20% of the American population). It would be impossible to provide any blanket statement of agreement on a policy issue for any group of 70 million people—particularly the diverse, opinionated, and fiercely independent generation I am proud to be a part of. A huge portion of us aren't even old enough to vote yet, and we as a generation have a ways to go before any sweeping generalization can be made about our collective generational opinions, but we already are breaking the mold with where we stand on the issues. We've been living in the upside down—but it's where we grow from here that will leave our generation's legacy.

Gen Z deserves real solutions to the big problems our culture faces day in and day out. You may not even realize it yet, but as a generation, we've far too often been presented with only one side of the political coin for policies and perspectives. In 2024, we have an opportunity and an obligation alike to embrace objective truth, true empathy for those around us, and hope for our future by courageously embracing conservativism for ourselves.

So, Gen Z Is Super Gay...

In early 2022, a Gallup poll was conducted on how U.S. adults would self-identify their gender and sexuality, and everyone (I mean *everyone*) was shocked by its results. For the first time in history, one in five adults within a generation self-identified as LGBTQ+—and that number is only expected to go up. I'm sure you can guess which generation it was.

When analyzing Gallup's findings, I was intrigued after discovering that the percentage of adults self-identifying as LGBTQ+ has essentially doubled from generation to generation. While 2.6% of baby boomers identified as such, that figure jumped to 4.2% for Gen X, a staggering 10.5% for millennials, and an unprecedented 20.8% for Gen Z. Jeff Jones, author of the Gallup poll, shared with Axios that he believes in the near future, 10-15% of the adult American population could identify as LGBTQ.[7]

While I was initially surprised by the figure itself, the sentiment didn't shock me. In the past few years alone, gender and sexuality has become perhaps the most discussed issue in American culture. We could spend an entire book unpacking where we're going on these issues alone, but generally speaking, it's important to note that Gen Z hasn't been exposed to the newfound language of gender theory for very long. During our early childhood years, pronouns were nothing more than a curriculum module in English class—not a subject of daily conversation. While I had the luxury of going through an entire school year wearing pretty much nothing but boys' basketball shorts from Target, Aeropostale graphic T-shirts, and bulky skater sneakers without anyone assuming I identified as a boy, today's kids aren't so lucky.

Gender theory and the concept of a malleable gender identity is a powerful message that spread faster than wildfire, and in the 2020s it is dominating our national attention span, from our TikTok for-you pages to official statements from the White House. Truly, I believe that it has become the fastest transforming conversation in American history, forever changing our culture in its wake. What began as a harmless "boys can play with Barbie, girls can play with G.I. Joe" sentiment almost overnight became a generational programming of Gen Z by those responsible for raising and educating us: we were told that gender is not a fixed biological reality, but a nebulous feeling that can change on a day-by-day basis.

Particularly following the nationwide debate surrounding same-sex marriage (which I should note is more controversial for Gen Z than you may think...only half of us believe that gay and lesbian couples having access to legal marriage is good for society, according to Pew Research), the LGBTQ+ conversation transformed in an instant.[8] It seemed the moment the Supreme Court gavel hit the desk to determine a marital right for same-sex couples in *Obergefell v. Hodges* in 2015, the issue of gay marriage disappeared into our history books. Now, our generational battlefield is marked by chromosomes versus pronouns, binary versus fluid, and biology versus emotion.

Today, our generation is told there are an unlimited number of genders, and anything can be our "pronouns." Literally. I mean *anything*. The longer I scroll through TikTok, the more insanity I come across, from people calling themselves "it/its" to using "they/demon" pronouns.[9] Yes. DEMON. Polling has found "the share of U.S. adults who are transgender is particularly high among adults younger than 25," and that "about 5% of young adults in the U.S. say their gender is different from their sex assigned at birth."[10] Teachers spend classroom time unpacking the meaning of pronouns, and school libraries are stocking pornographic sex manuals encouraging a societal departure from gender roles. Women have now become "birthing people" or "people who menstruate" in order to be more inclusive, and our college campuses stock tampons in the men's restrooms so as not to assume who is getting their period.

While we're presented with a glossy, glittery rainbow symbolizing ultimate inclusion and a celebration of our diversity—which couldn't possibly be a bad thing, right?—the true nature of today's anything-goes gender theory involves a dark side for Gen Z, too. Be it a teenage girl being sexually assaulted in school bathrooms accepting of trans identities in Loudoun County, Virginia, to NCAA Ivy League swimmers being exposed to male genitalia while competing against Will (Lia) Thomas, who now dominates the collegiate women's swimming pool as a trans woman instead of slumming it as a man, gender theory is ushering in real consequences that are anything *but* inclusive. Gen Z girls are beaten by men in our sports, harassed by creepy guys in bathrooms, and groomed online by popular influencers who would do anything to end the outdated, antiquated binary of gender forevermore. But sure, go off about how we live in the most feminist chapter of world history.

The narrative has gone so far, in fact, that many believe transgender identities and coming out as nonbinary has become the latest social contagion taking over America. In her bestselling book *Irreversible Damage*, journalist Abigail Shrier describes the "transgender craze seducing our daughters" as the latest social contagion plaguing teen girls. While high school hallways used to house quiet struggles with eating disorders and depression, teens today are pressured into running away from their very DNA and basic biology in order to fit in with the skyrocketing percentage of Gen Zers identifying themselves with "cool" labels like "trans" or "nonbinary." What should be shocking medical professionals everywhere is instead pushed on parents and their pressured children alike. Most doctors, therapists, and school administrators repeat a narrative to families that if they don't immediately affirm their daughter's new gender identity and pronouns, she will inevitably commit suicide from the emotional trauma of her newfound gender dysphoria (despite suicide rates not being affected by hormone or surgical transition at all). Today, Shrier warns, gender transition is a widespread social concern for any parent of a teenager, and it only seems to be picking up steam.[11]

Planned Parenthood has begun expanding their business model beyond abortion in a post-*Roe* America to become one of the largest providers of hormones to teenagers desiring to transition. Their own websites boast their ability to hand out these life-altering and often chemically castrating drugs like candy, telling interested teens they can get a prescription within the same day with no consultation with a therapist confirming gender dysphoria.[12] Intent on profiting off population decline, they're shifting their focus away from abortion and toward chemical castration of teens before they ever get pregnant to begin with.

A former pediatric transgender clinic worker in Missouri recently spoke out against their Mendelian practices, sharing her observations of licensed medical professionals providing hormone prescriptions to children with no diagnosis of gender dysphoria and often a history of other psychological problems. Queer and "politically to the left of Bernie Sanders" herself, Jamie Reed shared her experience feeling deeply uncomfortable with the practices of the clinic refusing to confirm a viable diagnosis of gender dysphoria for a barrage of teens who, chances are, will reunite with their biological gender identity by adulthood. Reading her first-person account of working at the Washington University Transgender Center at St. Louis Children's Hospital titled "I Thought I Was Saving Trans Kids. Now I'm Blowing the Whistle" is enough to make anyone stop dead in their tracks. Rather than pushing castrating and life-altering drugs to teens who often had yet to undergo puberty, she felt compelled to voice an alternative approach offering psychological support to these kids in crisis—only to be silenced by the doctors and nurses running the clinic and labeled a bigoted extremist for not going along with today's ever-changing demands of gender theory. Jamie says this type of authoritarian medicine poisoning America's youth is happening nationwide, and if we don't act immediately, it may be too late for thousands of kids who deserve better.[13]

As a side note, I thank God every day I had the luxury of experiencing childhood when I did. As you already know, my fifth-grade year will forever be identified in my memory with boys' clothes and skater shoes over pink frilly dresses and kitten heels. Throughout middle school, all of my friends were boys in an attempt to escape the vicious nature of preteen girlhood—goodness. Middle school girls are insufferable. By high school, my favorite thing to do every summer was to spend days or even weeks camping in the woods without showering at summer camp in the Colorado mountains rather than suntanning at the pool or shopping at the mall. Today, any one of those would serve as a flashing marquee sign to teachers, camp counselors, or just about anyone else that I could be a boy trapped in a girl's body. At the time, they simply signaled that it was okay to be a girl who wore basketball shorts, played video games with her drama-free guy friends, and loved playing outside.

The truth is, I could write an entire book on the state of gender alone in America today. If it's not yet obvious, this has become one of our most passion-driven issues because we are constantly bombarded with the narrative that unless we embrace radical gender theory and encourage children to transition immediately, we are evil extremists whose anger and bigotry have no place in society. We are told that in order to truly care about our peers, we should shove them into irreversible hormone regimens and even surgeries. With very few people foiling this powerful narrative in the court of public opinion, far too many buy into it.

Yet the incredible part of it all is this: in the midst of perhaps the greatest social propaganda campaign in modern history, Gen Z hasn't entirely bought into today's gender theory—and you don't have to, either. Countering the onslaught of coordinated lies and delusion is perhaps the bravest thing our generation could embrace, yielding true empowerment and love for one another in a very broken time.

Countless courageous voices like Chloe Cole have taken to social media to share their experiences of being swindled by the Alphabet Mafia—today a common nickname for those encouraging child gender transition on TikTok—only to detransition back to their biological gender, seeking to offer hope to those struggling with the societal pressure to transition. Speaking out to tens of thousands of followers on social media, Chloe detailed her harrowing journey battling with confusion over her gender, warning others about the potential to be duped by the pediatric gender industry. She was prescribed hormone blockers and testosterone starting at age 13, underwent a double mastectomy at age 15, and detransitioned back to her biological gender at 16. When her parents expressed concern for potential consequences of transitioning so young, doctors asked, "Would you rather have a dead daughter or an alive son?"[14]

LGBTQ+ influencers, creators, and commentators have even started using their platforms to speak out against the lies of the modern Pride movement seeking to exploit children for financial and political gain, from trans YouTuber Blaire White to podcaster Christian Walker and many others detaching themselves from the movement at large. Their videos and podcast episodes serve as a refreshing change of pace and counterperspective to the overwhelming narrative that has pummeled our generation more with each passing day. Groups like Gays Against Groomers have taken the media by storm, aimed at curbing the misinformation hiding behind the guise of progressive inclusion that's strategically lying to Gen Z.

Confronting the powerful tsunami of propaganda aiming to destroy gender as we know it for my generation is a difficult task, but at the very least, it gives us an opportunity to understand why we're so overwhelmingly seduced by modern gender theory. Voices like those I just mentioned are changing hearts and minds within our generation daily, but we have to be willing to speak the truth to our peers longing so desperately for meaning and identity. There is absolutely room for a change of generational perspective when it comes to gender and sexuality—if we are only willing to confront the loudest voices in culture.

WTF Is the Economy?!

In the 2022 election cycle, Republicans across the board believed a massive "Red Wave" was coming for the Biden administration and the Democratic Party, largely because of how dismal the economy was. The price of gasoline had regularly reached record highs, groceries became too expensive for any average American, and the dream of owning a home continued disappearing for more and more young people. No matter our political affiliation, every one of us felt the tight strain of Bidenomics, and Republican leadership knew it could be a powerful means to rally voters in the upcoming midterm elections—after all, the economy historically had always been the most powerful issue to mobilize voters in years past.

Republicans believed they could convince the nation their wallet was on the ballot. But when no red wave happened, it came as a shock to many around the country, Republican and Democrat alike—but it's easy to understand why. While the Right tried to tug at your pocketbook, the Left tugged at young voters' heartstrings. Democrats were able to successfully convince Gen Z their *life* was on the ballot, not just their wallet.

I spent the evening of November 8, 2022, feeling overwhelmingly frustrated with those angry at the supposed "disappearance" of the inevitable red wave. Throughout the past year on my livestream and in my social media content, I had been warning conservatives across America that the only way to win over Gen Z for any election cycle was not to rely on our anger over the economy, but to expand our messaging to include social issues Gen Z deeply cares about on both sides of the aisle. We needed to expand our messaging beyond economic issues to include social issues from abortion to the environment and everything in between. That's not to say we aren't frustrated when the economy is bad, but in truth, it's impossible to rally our generation behind building a stronger economy because we fundamentally don't understand the economy to begin with.

How could we, when our entire educational experience is structured around keeping us financially illiterate? Like most Gen Zers, I spent years in school learning how to type, the rules of kickball in PE, and the Pythagorean theorem, but not once was I ever required to learn about how to pay my taxes or what a mortgage was. Today, according to a survey from Investopedia, only 46% of us feel confident about our financial knowledge, a figure lower than baby bomers, Gen X, and millennials alike. Paying taxes ranks as one of our top financial concerns as a generation—perhaps because we feel so little confidence in knowing how to pay them.[15]

The economy has consistently been a roller coaster ride throughout our life, from the tightening of America's pocketbooks with the dawn of the war on terror to the 2008 housing crisis; the high of the Trump presidency offering more job opportunities and cheaper goods and services to the crash of our COVID-19 response shuttering businesses and schools. We've *always* been told it's unlikely that we'll be able to afford a down payment on a home, and like the majority of my generation, I have experienced a year-to-year rent increase to adjust for inflation every year since I moved into my first apartment at nineteen. In Biden's America, we are consistently gaslit by our nation's leadership about living in a "strong" economy—never mind the fact that the price of goods and services has skyrocketed under his presidency. In mid-2022, gasoline prices had shot up 107.4%, and groceries cost 14.6% more than when Biden took office in 2021.[16] Unfortunately, we feel the tightening of our wallets, but we don't connect the dots to poor economic management by those in Washington—especially when countless @potus social media posts center around creating more jobs than any other president in history or a booming economy.[17] Tough to disagree with the facts, when you're most often only presented with one side of the story, particularly given our overwhelming consumption of news and current events through our social media feeds.

As a result, Gen Z consistently ranks economic issues far lower than social issues when it comes to our political priorities. While abortion, the environment, and gender equality consistently rank among top issues for all Gen Zers (regardless of partisanship), the economy regularly falls in our priority list. That's not to say the economy and strong economic management aren't important, or that it shouldn't be a priority for anyone running for office, but in order to win over the soon-to-be-largest voter block in American history, conservatives can no longer assume inflation will captivate constituents. Gen Z is redefining how we market ideas to voters, and it starts with discussing how socially someone will work to transform America for the better.

Moreover, it's time for us to embrace opportunities to understand why the economy matters. While tax policy, GDP growth, and inflation aren't nearly as flashy as gender theory or abortion, they are important for us to take ownership over our generation's road to success. Understanding economics isn't just for buttoned-up, suit-clad elderly men—it's a crucial skill that will assist in our entrepreneurship, contribution to the greater American economy, and providing for our families to come. You don't need to rely on your teachers and professors to educate you on the ins and outs of financial policy (chances are, you aren't going to get the education you need there anyway). Simply watching instructional YouTube videos and following financial gurus on social media are a great way to start. Let's work together to learn what we can where we need to grow, while empowering those older than us to expand their messaging along the way.

Not Just for Greta

Growing up in the mountains of Colorado, I have had a deep love for the great American outdoors for as long as I can remember. To this day, my favorite way to spend a day would be hiking in the middle of the wilderness, fly-fishing on a serene river, surfing in our beautiful oceans, skiing through deep powder, or simply enjoying our nation's public lands and national parks. Lacing up your hiking boots and throwing on a puffy jacket was never a "lefty" thing to do where I grew up, and to this day, I am proud to be labeled "granola" by my friends who grew up in big cities. All summer long, you'll find Chacos on my feet as I compete with my siblings to get the best "Chaco tan," and I spend most weekends figuring out how I can play outside in any way possible.

As I have grown up and found a voice for Gen Z in the political sphere, I have discovered that perhaps the largest generational divide in American politics has grown over how we care for our environment and what role we ought to play in conserving our nation's resources for generations to come. While we all may roll our eyes at the outrageousness of Greta Thunberg and the billionaires who lecture us on environmental impact while flying massive private jets to Davos, Switzerland, every year for the World Economic Forum, environmentalism and conservation are not partisan issues for Gen Z. Period. Nor should they be.

Today, Gen Zers consistently rank the environment as one of our top issues culturally and politically that we seek to address. We are far more likely than those older than us to say the earth is warming due to human activity—54% according to Pew

Research Center, to be precise—and we're looking for stronger leadership on both sides of the aisle to tackle the problems the environment faces daily.[18] In 2022, politically conservative environmental action group American Conservation Coalition, led by Forbes 30 Under 30 recipient Benji Backer, found that "Americans aged 18-30 are generally unhappy with the direction our country is headed, with 53% of respondents saying we're on the wrong track."[19]

While many older than us assume our generation's heart for the environment is a result of our abundant ties to leftism—it's time for them to think again. According to Pew Research, 49% of young Republicans and conservative-leaning Gen Zers believe "action to reduce the effects of climate change needs to be prioritized today," compared with 37% of Gen Xers and 26% of baby boomers. That "action" doesn't necessarily look like passing the overwhelmingly problematic Green New Deal, mandating electric vehicles, or banning gas stoves, but rather investing in green technology innovation and prioritizing American energy independence with cleaner environmental impact. Further, our desire for environmental impact transcends government action and corporate policies—two-thirds of us believe ordinary Americans are doing too little to care for the environment as well.[20]

Gen Z's natural heart and passion for conservation perhaps stem from our collective love of the great outdoors. Despite the cultural assumption that we spend all our time with eyes glued to screens, the majority of our generation craves an unplugged day free from screens in the great American outdoors. In 2019, a Statista report found nearly 60% of Gen Z participated in outdoor activities—making Gen Z the most outdoorsy generation in the United States.[21] Side note—guess who encompassed the lowest rate of participation in outdoor activities generationally? Baby boomers...the same people who assume we can't go five minutes without our phones. Especially during the COVID-lockdown era, our generation found a renewed sense of wonder in exploring the great outdoors when we quite literally couldn't do anything else. Our deep love of hiking, camping, skiing, surfing, rock climbing, you name it, has driven a deep desire to care for our nation's most beautiful places, ensuring every generation after us has the opportunity to play the way we love to. America is our home, and it's our obligation to care for it.

As our generation falls in love with the environment, we're rediscovering our nation's roots (no pun intended) of conservation. Far from being a Sierra Club, hippie-in-a-VW-bus, Greta Thunberg leftist social movement, environmentalism in America can trace its roots back to President Abraham Lincoln through the vein of conservative politics. (Though honestly, I would still love to drive a bright orange VW bus.) Conservatives caring for the environment throughout our nation's history was never on my radar, even as a "granola" conservative myself—but much to my surprise, conservation really did originate with those seeking to conserve, not just our political values or system of governance, but the beautiful places we're obligated to protect.

In fact, it was President Abraham Lincoln, America's first Republican president, who set aside the first public land in our nation's history in the Yosemite Valley.[22] Conservative president Theodore Roosevelt, often referred to as "the conservation president," is considered the father of the National Park Service through the Antiquities Act and one of the most pro-environment political leaders in American history (plus, he was just an absolute legend to boot).[23] Say what you want about the guy (and, frankly, the agency), but it was Republican president Richard Nixon who established the Environmental Protection Agency in 1970.[24] More recently, President Trump left a strong environmental legacy during his term in office by renewing the Clean Power Plan,[25] establishing the One Trillion Trees Interagency Council,[26] championing and signing the Great American Outdoors Act as the largest modern investment in the National Park Service, and more.[27]

Young conservatives championing the environment isn't a departure from right-of-center political policy: it's a return to our roots throughout American history. Turns out, conservatives *conserve*—it's right there in our name. Environmental protection and a policy on conservation are essential to winning over Gen Z, and we'll continue demanding more from our elected officials on the issue from both sides of the aisle.

Character versus Color

It goes without saying that America has taken a steep departure from Martin Luther King Jr.'s dream of living in a nation valuing the content of someone's character over the color of their skin. Race has become one of the top political issues Gen Z feels passionate about in the 2020s, with roughly two-thirds of us saying that black Americans are treated less fairly than white Americans in this country.[28] Whether you believe it's true or not, it's a widespread belief within our generation that is driving many of our choices both politically and culturally, and it is allowing the Left to thrive by championing the messaging on the issue nationwide.

Honestly, it's hard to imagine why we feel this way (not), when critical race theory has fundamentally transformed the way our generation approaches race relations. Rather than being taught to look beyond skin color and focus on one's content of character, Gen Z's belief that people are treated differently on the basis of race centers entirely around our society's obsession with the content of melanin in our skin. Every February, nearly every major corporation and politician panders to the black community by supporting the pro-Marxist organization Black Lives Matter. For the record, this organization has called for the disruption of the "nuclear family structure," and one movement leader was even accused of stealing ten million dollars for personal use.[29] The *New York Times'* propaganda-style *1619 Project*, seeking to claim America's very foundation centered around the horrors of slavery, has been publicly debunked by countless historians—yet still has seeped into the lineup of public school curriculum nationwide. Colleges and universities have reinstituted segregated dormitories, black-only spaces on campus, and segregated graduation ceremonies in a shocking return to what remarkably resembles Jim Crow policies. This time, though, we hide behind the label of leftism and call it "progressive" and "empowering."

Like gender theory, critical race theory has become a powerful tool to rally the emotions of Gen Z through a manipulated sense of compassion. We are told the only way to support minorities or truly care about historic oppression is to embrace the radical Marxism pushed by BLM, Inc., or empower "mostly peaceful" (*cough cough*, violent) protests in the inner city. The unfortunate reality few are willing to expose is this: critical race theory is hell-bent on manifesting further division between racial groups in America and around the world. If we truly want to end racism as we know it, it starts with unifying us all, regardless of skin color—not dividing. Until fearless voices like Candace Owens dedicated themselves to speaking up above the pro-BLM crowd, it's likely no one in our lives dared to rise above the narrative and speak the truth. Gen Z is constantly surrounded by the noise of racially divisive politicians, social media posts, school curriculum, and more—and it's time for those in power to recapture Martin Luther King Jr.'s dream again.

Our post-modern approach to race relations has entirely abandoned the dream of the American Civil Rights Movement for a future in which the human race means far more than the race of the individual. Through our misplaced compassion, we have financed and fueled movements dedicated to further racial division, rioting and destruction of private property, and even overt segregation. The leaders of these movements attack and belittle minorities who don't adhere to rigid leftism. They call for an end to our most beautiful human institution—the nuclear family. They even misuse millions of dollars in donations to end racism to fly in private jets and purchase multimillion-dollar homes.[30] They aren't interested in ending racism or building bridges; they're hoping to further division as much as possible in order to continue turning a profit. It's time for our generation to open our eyes to the shallow I of progress propagated by the so-called anti-racists of the political Left, abandoning false activism for true empowerment and unity.

The Post-*Roe* Generation

In the 2020s, perhaps Gen Z's single most important political issue has become abortion. Particularly since the overturning of *Roe v. Wade* with the *Dobbs v. Jackson* Supreme Court decision in the summer of 2022, abortion has recaptured the nation as one of our most contentious and divisive debates, and it's no secret that the pro-abortion lobby has dedicated countless time, energy, and resources to impacting public opinion (particularly of Gen Z) toward their side.

Today, America's largest abortion provider (Planned Parenthood, in case you didn't know) has become a behemoth of public policy and political power beyond the services they provide in neighborhood clinics nationwide. Shaping the formation of sex-ed curriculum in K-12 schools all over America, Planned Parenthood began impacting my generation's opinions on abortion from an early age.[31] A shocking number of Planned Parenthood abortion facilities are down the street from major college campuses, and you'll often find representatives of the organization tabling on campus handing out free flyers, stickers, and buttons to students reminding them of the availability of abortion at a moment's notice just mere steps away.

Our nation's attitude toward abortion has fundamentally transformed even within my lifetime, largely thanks to the influence of powerful groups like Planned Parenthood capturing our attention in our earliest years of life, pulling the purse strings for our elected representatives on the campaign trail, and manipulating social media and the entertainment industry. What used to be the commonly repeated talking points of "safe, legal, and rare," a harrowing choice no woman should ever have to confront, and something we should prevent quickly, became something worthy of celebration. Today, America all-out glorifies abortion. We have sparkly, aesthetic graphics on our social media feeds championing abortion procedures. Miley Cyrus licks a rainbow-sprinkled cake reading "ABORTION IS HEALTH-CARE" as a paid collaboration with Planned Parenthood on Instagram, and it's shared by millions.[32] "Shout your abortion" has become a social campaign encouraging women to be proud of the decision they made to end their child's life, with the slogan "WE WILL AID + ABET ABORTION" plastered in caps on their website.[33] I even recently came across a TikTok video with someone getting ready to throw an "abortion shower" in lieu of a baby shower, with shooters of alcohol and a heating pad to comfort a no-longer-expectant mother.

Agree with it or not—abortion has become normal in America. Long gone are the "safe, legal, and rare" days of decades past. Instead, Gen Z is targeted, indoctrinated, and all-out culturally shoved into supporting abortion, or else, at the risk of appearing to be "anti-woman" in today's culture of modern feminism.

Never mind, of course, that supporting the abortion lobby in America today has become about the least *actually* feminist thing you could possibly do. In the wake of *Roe*'s reversal, major corporations like Amazon, Mastercard, and Tesla began lining up around the block to announce they'd cover the cost of traveling out of state to obtain an abortion for their female employees. How progressive, *right*? When you really think about it, though, it's a whole hell of a lot more expensive to provide better maternity leave and schedule flexibility for new mothers than a weekend away at a five-star hotel and a singular surgery.

Last year, the Biden administration announced chemical abortion pills would be permitted for distribution in pharmacies like Walgreens, CVS, and Rite Aid—how progressive, *right*? Sure, until you consider the medical realities that chemical abortion pills are four times more dangerous and ten times more deadly for pregnant women than surgical abortion, that chemical abortion pills are poisoning our nation's water and soil, and that they are emotionally devastating for young women who are told taking these pills is "just like taking Tylenol," only to find themselves holding their child in the bathtub and flushing her down the toilet.

In America today, we're told the only way to uplift and support women in crisis—financial hardship, emotionally and physically abusive relationships, or potential single parenthood—is to empower her to end the life of her child, who would inevitably be impossible to care for when it's just too hard. How progressive, *right*? Planned Parenthood in particular preys on these women who are facing difficulty by convincing them of just that—and making money off of them in the process. Meanwhile, foiling the roughly 600 abortion clinics in America are more than 3,000 pro-life pregnancy centers that go above and beyond to *actually* assist women in crisis. Providing free prenatal care, hosting baby showers and diaper drives, fundraising for rent and mortgage assistance, and even finding free babysitting aren't things to profit from for these centers, but simply a part of the culture of life the pro-life movement is building, one family at a time.

When you consider the influence and impact of the abortion lobby—easily among the most powerful groups shaping culture and policy in America today—on Gen Z, it's no wonder that the majority of us would call ourselves pro-abortion. Recently, the Public Religion Research Institute (PRRI) found that 72% of 18- to 29-year-old Americans support the legality of abortion in all or most cases. Of course they do—it was Planned Parenthood who taught us sex ed, encouraging us to utilize their services if (God forbid) we'd ever need to. It's Planned Parenthood who has set up abortion clinics within walking distance of our college campuses (87.6% of the 563 Planned Parenthood facilities in operation are located within five miles of a college campus, for the record).[34] It's Planned Parenthood who finances pro-abortion politicians and catchy social media campaigns with beautiful graphic designs to make abortion trendy and cool.

Incredibly, though, like every polarizing issue facing America today, Gen Z is not totally sold on the abortion lobby. Like gender theory, critical race theory, and more, we remain inherently skeptical as a generation—especially on topics so overmarketed to us. Thanks to the work of individual journalists and pro-life organizations, we're starting to learn for the first time what an abortion procedure actually is. We're wrestling with ideological debate on the subject day in and day out on our TikTok feeds, starting clubs on our high school and college campuses, and seeking dialogue that culture says we should run away from.

We've been reminded of the overwhelming toll the abortion industry has taken on our generation in particular. The shocking reality is this: of the 63 million children who have been killed at the hands of the abortion industry, 26 million were Gen Zers, according to Live Action.[35] That shakes out to about one-third of my generation who isn't here today, because they never got the opportunity to be here. That's a group of people greater than the entire population of every single individual state, minus Texas and California.

While the overwhelming majority of Gen Zers would consider themselves to be pro-abortion, it's much more nuanced than we think. In fact, pro-life organizations across the movement have labeled Gen Z the Post-*Roe* Generation, and we're living up to that name. A recent survey conducted by Students for Life of America on young voters surrounding the Biden administration's handling of abortion policy uncovered shocking results. A majority of respondents said they supported banning abortion after a baby's heartbeat can be found; 75% said they favor restrictions on abortion procedures; 40% want abortion to be either illegal entirely, or legal only in the cases of rape, incest, or when a mother's life is endangered; and 60% said they oppose the legality of abortion through all nine months of pregnancy.[36]

Abortion is easily one of the most, if not the most, controversial issue of our time, but it's something we care deeply about. It's tempting to run away from this conversation at every opportunity, particularly knowing how emotionally entangled so many hearts have become on the subject throughout the past several decades. While most people older than us strategically avoid discussing the topic for fear of ruffling feathers, Gen Z is hungry for dialogue and ready to change our hearts and minds.

We're already making waves as the post-*Roe* generation, unafraid to challenge the status quo by fighting for human rights even when it's unpopular. While the culturally "normal" thing to do today may be to keep your head down and avoid ruffling feathers, America has lost too many innocent children at the hands of staying silent. Our generation deserves more than the empty lies of abortion and devastating physical and psychological damage that has wreaked havoc on far too many of us already. Women in crisis deserve more than a quick-fix yielding decades of emotional distress. We deserve to celebrate motherhood and promote human rights for us all.

Calling yourself pro-life isn't evil, outdated, or bigoted. It's the most noble identity our generation could possibly embrace.

See Ya, Cancel Culture

Perhaps the most impactful cultural movement of our teenage and young adult years has been cancel culture, the push to destroy the livelihood of anyone who fails to live up to our constantly changing societal expectations and what is considered "politically correct" on a day-by-day basis. No one is immune to becoming the next head on the chopping block: say the wrong thing, tweet something insensitive (or have something you tweeted ten years ago become uncovered), or vote for the wrong guy, and you might just be next to have your social media accounts deleted, your job terminated, or your friends walk out of your life.

Cancel culture has generated an environment of fear in which we feel the need to self-censor, follow the crowd, and do what is "acceptable" according to the culture of the day. We have created a society that serves as a vacuum without grace, redemption, or growth. Far too often, I see Gen Z blamed as the catalyst for cancel culture's dramatic impact on America, when in reality we are actively fighting against it.

I will never forget being a student on my college campus at Colorado State University and coming across an article in our student newspaper listing words that the administration had suddenly deemed "canceled." It appeared a faculty board had convened without any input from students, deciding our fragile personalities required mass censorship on our public university campus in order for us to thrive as young adults. Seemingly overnight, without even asking us if we were offended by these words and phrases, they compiled a document called the CSU "Inclusive Language Guide."[37] I published the guide in its entirety in my last book, *Frontlines*, and discussed my experience ruffling a few feathers from my alma mater's faculty lineup discussing the guide on the news and social media. Trust me when I say that this document would floor you. Included in the list are words and phrases like "cakewalk," "crazy," "eenie meenie miney moe," "peanut gallery," "rule of thumb," and even "food coma." All of which were supposedly racist, sexist, or just generally bigoted in some way, shape, or form.

Those inclusions in the list were comical, but others were not: "male/female," "straight," "Mr./Mrs.," and even the word

"America" were listed as words to be avoided at all costs, at the risk of offending someone. Because how dare we assume America is the name of our country, be proud to call ourselves Americans, or suggest that one could be considered male or female.

What was an insane (oops, better be careful, that's probably on the list) document compiled by Far Left faculty and administrators on my campus soon became the norm in higher education. Google "university inclusive language guide" today, and you'll find results from some of our nation's most prestigious academic institutions—Northwestern, Boston University, the University of Washington, UC Davis, UC Berkeley, and even Columbia. Gen Zers nationwide have been strategically taught to self-censor by Gen X and boomer faculty hell-bent on imposing cancel culture on us from our first moment on campus.

These guides are just one example of how extreme cancel culture has become—as we've graduated from college, this culture has graduated with us and permeated America's corporate board rooms, our social media feeds, and even our financial institutions. Especially in the fear-driven era of COVID-19 and the rise of "mostly peaceful" protests organized by violent groups, America (oops again) has discovered just how far the cancellation police will go.

We live in a time where doctors could lose their license to practice medicine if they recommend an alternative treatment to the narrative of Dr. Anthony Fauci. Where you could lose access to your financial accounts as a small business owner if you share what their staff deems to be "misinformation." Where you may be fired from your job, lose your closest relationships with friends and family, or be expelled from school if you don't follow the crowd. It's unsurprising, then, that 62% of Americans today say they have political views they're afraid to publicly share, according to the Cato Institute.[38]

Incredibly, despite being blamed for instigating cancel culture, it is Gen Z who is overwhelmingly rejecting it. While millennials report the highest rates of supporting cancel culture, Gen Z is the most likely generation in America to oppose it. A Morning Consult poll recently found that 55% of Gen Zers "express negative views" about cancel culture, while only 36% of millennials do. While boomers and Gen Xers alike tend to blame Gen Z for catalyzing cancel culture, only 8% of my generation supports it. Fascinatingly, as you break down Gen Z even further, it's the younger cohort of my generation that stands most firmly against canceling those different from themselves: 59% of 13- to 16-year-olds, to be exact.[39]

These aren't just poll numbers on a website. America is observing Gen Z rejecting cancel culture in real time in a practical sense, too. In the last few years, cancellation has raged with all its might through popular culture—but we are fighting back and opening the door to redemption again.

When country music singer Morgan Wallen uttered a racial slur aloud in a leaked 2021 video online during a night of partying with his friends, everyone was sure his career was done. He was uninvited from every major music awards ceremony, stripped of PR opportunities, and chastised by the loudest voices for making a mistake. After apologizing on numerous occasions, he was rarely seen in the public eye—easily a path to a fizzling career, especially when this all took place just three weeks after releasing *Dangerous: The Double Album,* which debuted at number one on the *Billboard* 200 Albums chart. A promising kickoff to 2021-turned-inevitable end of his career proved to be a turning point for Wallen.[40]

Instead of giving in to the cancel culture mob, he sought genuine forgiveness from his fan base and admitted to wrongdoing, expressing his regret and desire for redemption—something that never would have been out of the ordinary in culture before the 2020s, but today is a rare allowance by those seeking the destruction of anyone who thinks differently from themselves.

Shockingly, Wallen's *Dangerous* stayed atop the Billboard album charts for seven more weeks at number 1 after the video's release and spent literally dozens of weeks charting in the top 10. In fact, he even broke the record for the longest Top 10 album run by a single artist. He performed worldwide to sold-out crowds for nearly every night of his *Dangerous* tour, and built a massive, loyal following of millions across social media platforms.

In 2023, Wallen released a triple album, *One Thing at a Time*, again instantly breaking countless Billboard records: most streams ever for a country album in a single week, biggest streaming week for any album in 2023 upon release, and first artist of any genre to notch over thirty Hot 100 hits in the same week.[41] If you would have asked anyone in the wake of a video using a racial slur if an artist would have the capacity to surpass the streaming records of Drake and Taylor Swift, the answer would have been "absolutely not." Incredibly, though, a single mistake surrounded by record-breaking music isn't a career ender for Wallen's Gen Z fan base, who has rallied around the artist with undying support since his apology and isn't going anywhere anytime soon.

Lesson learned? If you made a mistake, just apologize for it—while the media and a small handful of cancel-culture-obsessed maniacs may hold it over your head, Gen Zers are reinstituting redemption in America again.

Throughout the last year, perhaps no one has been more of a target for the cancel culture mob than Harry Potter author J. K. Rowling. After coming across an article about "people who menstruate," Rowling tweeted, "'People who menstruate'. I'm sure there used to be a word for those people. Someone help me out. Wumben? Wimpund? Woomud?" Immediately, she was labeled by Twitter users and activists worldwide as trans-phobic, anti-LGBTQ+, and bigoted, with many calling her a Trans-Exclusionary Radical Feminist (TERF).

Refusing to back down, Rowling has since repeatedly shared her views on social media that while all people are worthy of respect and love, trans women and biological women are inher-ently different, and culture's erasure of womanhood to accommo-date our progressive culture is about the least *actually* feminist thing one could do. She wrote in a subsequent thread on Twitter, "The idea that women like me, who've been empathetic to trans people for decades, feeling kinship because they're vulnerable in the same way as women—i.e., to male violence—'hate' trans peo-ple because they think sex is real and has lived consequences—is a nonsense. I respect every trans person's right to live any way that feels authentic and comfortable to them. I'd march with you if you were discriminated against on the basis of being trans. At the same time, my life has been shaped by being female. I do not believe it's hateful to say so."[42]

Hardly the evil, transphobic, and bigoted maniac the Left would like for you to believe, Rowling has spurred international dialogue on finding the balance between inclusion of others and empowering women. Sadly, she's also been the target of perhaps the most rabid online cancel culture campaign in the 2020s. Calls to boycott the Harry Potter franchise and throw away your favorite childhood books in order to deal a blow to the series' author have run rampant following her original tweet. A powerful narrative has even been spun that if you don't rid yourself of anything and everything Harry Potter, you are contributing to violent transphobia.

Last year, long-awaited open world video game *Hogwarts Legacy*'s upcoming release caused outcry from those seeking to cancel Rowling. TikTok videos circulating on the platform began garnering millions of views calling anyone who purchased the game transphobic through sobs and tears. One user posted a video saying, "If you buy the Hogwarts Legacy game, you are contributing to transphobia. Even if you consider yourself an ally, even if you yourself are trans, you are contributing to transphobia, and that is not an opinion—it's a fact."[43] I'm sorry, *WHAT*?! Apparently, the zealous anger toward someone who simply believes biological women and trans women are different warrants telling *literal trans people* they hate trans people if they buy a video game about wizards and witches.

You literally can't make this stuff up.

Like the calls to cancel Morgan Wallen, cancel culture's push to destroy J. K. Rowling has been anything but successful. Rowling herself has shared in interviews she does not consider herself to be canceled, revealing the entire controversy has only caused book sales to go up.[44] *Hogwarts Legacy* became an overnight success, selling over 12 million units and generating nearly $1 billion in sales in the first two weeks after the game's release.[45] In that same time period, Warner Bros. shared the game had already been played for over 280 million hours. *Newsweek* magazine ran a headline just days after the game's release reading "The 'Hogwarts Legacy' Boycott Failed."[46]

Of course, Rowling is no stranger to overcoming adversity herself in her personal life and as the creator of the Harry Potter franchise. In fact, she was turned down by twelve different publishers before finally signing to publish *Harry Potter and the Sorcerer's Stone*.[47] It takes an unimaginably determined person to push through countless trials and continue creating perhaps the most impactful franchise in my lifetime, and a series of angry tweets and emotional TikTok videos certainly won't spell her downfall.

More recently, YouTube's most followed creator, Jimmy Donaldson—known as MrBeast—found himself on the receiving end of cancel culture's calls for destruction. MrBeast spent the past few years building a gargantuan following of hundreds of millions of subscribers and followers across platforms, boasting more than 100 million subscribers on his primary YouTube channel alone. His feel-good fun videos embrace out-of-this-world challenges like "I Paid A Real Assassin To Try

To Kill Me," or "I Survived 50 Hours In Antarctica," or even "I Spent 50 Hours Buried Alive." My fiancé and I absolutely *love* MrBeast's channel—not just for the crazy videos he dares to make, but because he often goes out of his way to include his subscribers in his videos and regularly gives away money, cars, and more to help people who really need it. Instead of amassing personal wealth from his massive following, MrBeast has spent his career giving back to others, a particularly countercultural lifestyle particularly for content creators (especially for the biggest content creator on the face of the planet).

In early 2023, MrBeast released a new video on his channel entitled, "1,000 Blind People See for the First Time," during which he paid for eye surgery for more than 1,000 people suffering from blindness all over the world. The video partnered with SEE International, a nonprofit organization dedicated to their mission to treat and end preventable blindness. To date, they've treated millions of people around the world and were particularly excited to partner with the most followed content creator on earth bringing additional awareness to the issue.[48]

If you haven't already seen the video, you should: MrBeast's upbeat optimism coupled with the emotional reality of blind patients opening their eyes to sight is enough to pull at anyone's heartstrings. I remember watching the video for the first time with my fiancé shedding a tear and reflecting on how special it was that this person with unmatched influence was using his platform for good. Not only did he make the video, but he personally paid for each person's surgery and even gave away additional prizes worth tens of thousands of dollars to participants in the video. Quickly, though, it became obvious that not everyone shared the same reaction.

Some people on the internet labeled the video "charity porn," insinuating MrBeast was manipulating viewers by claiming he cared, while really fishing for likes and new subscribers.[49] Popular Twitch streamer and political commentator Hasan Piker condemned the video, saying it filled him with "rage" to watch.[50] He suggested influencers should not be used to fix problems like lack of access to health care and that videos like this one only enabled government inaction. During his stream, he said, "It is so extremely frustrating that it is up to one YouTube guy to decide to make content out of it when people who are too poor can't just fucking see."[51]

Online criticism of the video spread like wildfire, particularly on Twitter (seriously, I am convinced dreams just go to die over there). One user tweeted, "There is something so demonic about this and I can't even articulate what it is," amassing over 86,000 likes since its publication.[52] *Demonic?* Really?! I can't even begin to piece together what could be demonic about someone with resources choosing to spend them on helping blind people see... sounds like the opposite of demonic behavior to me, but maybe I'm just missing something.

So much controversy swirled surrounding the video online that MrBeast was eventually forced to respond, and I don't think he could have handled it any better. A few days after the video's release, he tweeted: "Twitter—Rich people should help others with their money. Me—Okay, I'll use my money to help people and I promise to give away all my money before I die. Every single penny. Twitter—MrBeast bad."[53]

Beyond this particular video, what you will never hear MrBeast boast about online is his philanthropic organization, Beast Philanthropy, founded in 2020 dedicated to "distributing food to underserved regions around Donaldson's hometown of Greenville, North Carolina" per Business Insider.[54] Since the organization's foundation, it has since launched humanitarian aid projects all over the globe, defined by the creator's signature optimism and sense of fun. The creator's Beast Philanthropy YouTube channel has shared updates on these projects in signature MrBeast style, recently posting videos like "We Built Wells in Africa!" and "Rebuilding Homes for Tornado Survivors." The channel's video "Giving 20,000 Shoes To Kids In Africa" has amassed over 16 million views, and "We Did 10,000 Random Acts of Kindness" perfectly embodies the overall message: anyone can make a positive difference in our broken world, no matter who you are or where you come from.[55] It's crazy to think today that a YouTuber from North Carolina provides a bigger influence than most celebrities, entrepreneurs, and politicians—maybe even the president of the United States—but I am consistently inspired by his heart to give back to others.

Why *anyone* would even remotely attempt to cancel MrBeast as one of the least controversial, most unifying figures of our time in an increasingly divided space of social media continues to baffle me—especially given the fact that he didn't do anything wrong, but was objectively kind and selfless! Yet again, to my joyful surprise, Gen Z showed up to shut down cancel culture rather than its latest targeted victim. Since the blindness video was published, he has gained tens of millions of subscribers on YouTube (plus tens of millions more on his other channels) and only grown in popularity. He's continued making fun videos encouraging people to laugh when we need it most and has given all of us a reminder that some things really are bigger than politics.

With each passing day, Gen Z is proving ourselves to value conversation over cancellation. We are choosing to engage with diverse opinions instead of siloing ourselves in with only those we agree with, eager to hear someone's point of view—even if it's dramatically different from our own. Our rejection of cancel culture's snowballing demands in modern society provides a fascinating social commentary surrounding our willingness to evolve: our fierce independence has created a pathway to change our hearts and minds on any given issue, given the opportunity. We have developed a set of generational values to date that may be different from those who came before us, but that's not to say we aren't willing to challenge our perspectives and points of view.

It's obvious, then, that conservatism should appeal to our generation with ease. While we may not often be confronted with conservative values and policies in a hyper-leftist echo chamber of modern culture, it's freedom and true empowerment driving our generational values. The shallow I of both promoted by the Left provides neither, but the promise of conservatism might. The truth is, the values that made the West great don't have to live in eras past, but can be brought into the future to truly empower our generation and everyone yet to come.

Gen Z is growing up and growing out of the echo chamber, ready to take on the modern world while seeking the truth.

CHAPTER 5

breaking the system

Ask any Gen Zer what the greatest TV show of all time is, and you'll find a good majority who respond with *Game of Thrones*. Maybe it's the intense political struggle for power, maybe it's the dragons, hell, maybe it's just the intensity of Kit Harington (*swoon*) as he portrays the legendary Jon Snow. Whatever it is, HBO's masterpiece adaptation of George R. R. Martin's fantasy world remains one of the most watched television series of all time.

If you haven't seen it, SHAME. SHAME. SHAME (iykyk). Just kidding. I hadn't seen it myself until 2021, despite being told repeatedly throughout college that I resembled the Mother of Dragons herself, Daenerys Targaryen. While I thought that sounded like a seriously badass title, I had no frame of reference for who she was or what the show was about, until I met my fiancé, who forced me to sit down and finally watch what I'd somehow avoided for the last several years. Like literally everyone else who takes the time to watch the show, I was hooked from the first episode, begging him to immediately play the next one, and binged the entire series in a span of a few weeks.

Without spoiling the plot, on the off chance you're part of the tiny population of people who haven't pretended they lived in Westeros and were vying for your seat on the Iron Throne yourself, a common theme throughout the show is the repeated cycle of power and culture. With each passing generation, a different house, or family, is vying for political and cultural control over everyone else to become the ultimate leader of the kingdom. Wars are fought, houses destroyed, and culture upended over and over again in order for someone to gain ultimate power and control. The wheel keeps spinning in perpetuity repeating the cycle...that is, until someone comes along who wants to stop the cycle entirely. Instead, they desire to "break the wheel," effectively destroying the system that has repeatedly destroyed society.

Complete side note—just stop watching after Season 7. You'll thank me later.

It's a messy process to "break the wheel" and change culture from the inside out, not just between the pages of George R. R. Martin's acclaimed literature or on our television screens, but even more so in real life. It's why many who work in American politics and commentary say we are living in the midst of a "culture war." It's not a euphemism or a silly expression to be thrown around hyperbolically to make a post go viral—it's an apt description of the severity we find ourselves in as we fight (sometimes, quite literally) for what the future of our culture is going to look like in America.

Like those in the Seven Kingdoms, Americans today are at a crucial turning point for our future—not just politically, but the future of our reality in its entirety. We have leaned into a completely perverted concept of right and wrong, truth and lies, progress and decline. Our trajectory today will determine if we fully embrace the upside down, or if we're able to right the ship. In the midst of this confusing chapter in history, one thing has become clear: Gen Z is ready to break the wheel.

Today, America's teenagers and young adults are looking around at the state of our Union and are collectively understanding that the culture our parents and predecessors have built for us is *not* the future we want to live in. We are refusing to embrace culture's prescribed pathways presented to us for success and happiness, be it obtaining a four-year degree in gender studies in order for us to find ourselves, climbing the corporate ladder through undying loyalty to the first company who hires us, or propping up the extreme ends of the two-party political system that our Founders warned against. Spoiler alert: American culture is becoming less "exceptional" by the day (and I am sharing this with you as someone who is deeply proud to be an American). The fast track to fame and fortune, health and happiness is not leading us where it's supposed to.

Rather than accepting our fate of mediocrity and misery, Gen Z is forging our own path, unafraid to challenge the status quo and intentionally "work smarter, not harder." We're changing culture from the inside out through every opportunity possible and creating a stronger future in the process. We're breaking the wheel to end the cycle of insanity that America has fallen into. Like every teenager feeling rebellious against their parents, we are rebelling against the world our parents built for us to pioneer our own avenue.

While far too many who came before us bemoan any trajectory into the future and instead argue it's time for America to return to the "good ol' days" of decades past, Gen Z understands a fundamental truth: we have shifted so substantially in culture and reality that "going back" isn't possible. Instead, it's time for us to embrace traditional values with a new-age twist, carrying us into the future instead of living in the past. After all, if life as we know it has fundamentally evolved into something unrecognizable, it's going to take a whole new playbook to get us back to reality.

Maybe breaking the wheel is exactly what we need.

A Division of the Republic

Just after the Revolutionary War as our young Founders reveled in their against-all-odds victory against the British Empire, they began to wisely predict the single most prominent threat to the new Republic. Knowing the universal resolve held by all Americans in conserving freedom, our earliest predecessors wisely knew the greatest threat to preserving our Union wouldn't come from abroad, but from right here at home. During his farewell address, our first president, George Washington, warned against the "domination of one [political] faction over another, sharpened by the spirit of revenge." His successor, President John Adams, shared a similar reflection: "a division of the republic into two great parties...is to be dreaded as the great political evil."[1]

While our forefathers had *just* secured their independence from a too-powerful regime, our Founding Fathers understood the great threat to freedom that could end the American experiment entirely. Far too often, they knew, people gravitate toward systems and people that uphold centralized power, giving up their liberty in exchange for security or convenience. More likely than not, destruction to this new Republic would not come from a foreign enemy, but the powerful internal political factions that have dictated the course of history through every nation the world has ever known.

The simple truth in these statements has carried through every chapter of our nation's history since its founding. In 1838, President Abraham Lincoln shared his belief that if we ever were to be destroyed, it would come from within: "It cannot come from abroad. If destruction be our lot, we must ourselves be its author and finisher. As a nation of freemen, we must live through all time, or die by suicide." Virtually every American president has echoed the warnings of Washington, Adams, and even later Lincoln—all while simultaneously playing into the partisan game of politics that (at least these days) has secured their spot in the Oval Office.

It seems, in the blink of an eye, our Founders' warnings became truth. The two major political parties control nearly every aspect of American politics today, determining who gets to run for office, where financial support is directed, and who holds the cards in Washington once elected. It's why the pendulum swings so ferociously when parties switch control in Congress or the White House, bills become stuck in the pipeline to laws, and action is likely never to be taken on issues like term limits.

Frighteningly, though, their political claws of control have grasped far more than even our systems of governance. News media has become partisan, with right-of-center voters more often than not watching Fox News, while left-wingers consume CNN or MSNBC. More than half of us on either side of the political coin say we wouldn't date someone who doesn't share our political views.[2] In 2020, NPR ran a story titled "'Dude, I'm Done': When Politics Tears Families and Friendships Apart," sharing stories from around the country about how partisanship had ripped cousins, siblings, and friends apart over how a ballot was cast.[3]

I hear countless stories every day of people who've lost their closest relationships after changing their minds or embracing a new perspective. I personally know several fellow content creators who no longer speak to even their parents or siblings after their family banished them for becoming conservative. After starting campus activism in college myself, I experienced the "Dude, I'm Done"-style excommunication from several of my friends. It seemed even those who'd been my best friends and closest confidants since preschool suddenly didn't know who I *really* was, even after almost twenty years of friendship. Though I simply had become more vocal in my values and decided to share them with others, never wavering in the things I've always believed in, they could no longer associate with me in any way, shape, or form—likely to avoid being on the receiving end of cultural backlash themselves.

The two-party system has driven a seismic shift in American values and our ability to continue living in a "United" States of America—so much so that not only are our voting patterns affected, but even our most intimate and personal relationships. We've even arrived at a time in our nation's history where those who vote differently than us are labeled evil, inhuman, and demonic. A 2022 study conducted by Pew Research found "growing shares in each party now describe those in the other party as more closed-minded, dishonest, immoral and unintelligent than other Americans...Today, 72% of Republicans regard Democrats as more immoral, and 63% of Democrats say the same about Republicans."[4] Long gone are the days we can safely assume we all might agree on where we're going as a nation but have differing opinions on how to get there—instead, we're all out dehumanizing those who vote and think differently than ourselves.

Incredibly, politicians on both sides remain publicly committed to a "united" nation and bringing Americans together in our increasingly divided country, but behind closed doors and in Washington they are forced to play the partisan game to stay in power. As a result, very little gets done to bring people together. Instead, we continue to divide as a nation further with each passing day. The Vanderbilt Unity Index, a measure of how unified or divided Americans are throughout modern history, has found our nation's unity has been steadily declining over the past three decades.[5] While Americans have never been fully unified in our beliefs—after all, mandating unified beliefs would be a stark departure from a free society—it begs the question what is left we *can* come together on without the dramatic influence of the two-party system, if anything.

The rise of Gen Z into the political sphere presents perhaps the greatest threat to the two major parties America has ever encountered, at least since our forefathers. Dubbed by many as the "politically homeless" generation, we are overwhelmingly rejecting the idea that the only choices concerning political leadership are associated with a red "R" or a blue "D."[6] Nor are we embracing America's existing third-party options, either—instead of trading the Republicans and Democrats for Libertarians or Green Party candidates, Gen Z is coupling our fierce cultural independence with our newfound political identity as we continue growing up.

Today, as you already know, over half of us are identifying ourselves as politically Independent, according to a recent Gallup poll. Moreover, nearly half of 18- to 49-year-olds wish there were more parties to choose from in American politics beyond the two-party powerhouses and our limited third-party alternatives, as Pew Research Center found.[7] It shows in how we're voting, too—while Gen Z often leans left in our voting patterns, we're trending more conservative over time and turning out to vote beyond expectations with every major national election—meaning we're showing up to make our voices heard and we're pulling America back toward the middle in the midst of increasing partisanship.

Gen Z is repeatedly gravitating toward candidates and policies that are not singularly owned by a party, but those that are willing to lead even when it's politically inconvenient. Instead of blindly backing a politician or ballot initiative based on the letter next to their name every November, we're reminding Washington that our government works for the people—not the other way around. If those in power want Gen Z's support, they are going to have to earn it through following through on far-too-often empty promises on the campaign trail, be willing to break free from party demands, and be able to prove how a policy is going to tangibly impact culture.

Better yet, we're refusing to wait for partisan politicians who have been in office for decades to finally wake up and change the system, so we're running for office ourselves. In 2022, Maxwell Frost (D-FL) became the first Gen Zer elected to the United States House of Representatives. At the same time, my friend and former White House colleague Karoline Leavitt was running to become the youngest person ever elected to Congress out of the great state of New Hampshire as a Republican. Truly, two people could not be more different—Maxwell has been described as a Green New Deal supporter and formerly worked as an activist for March for Our Lives, encouraging politicians to adopt drastic gun control measures.[8] Karoline worked as a communications staffer in the Trump White House and later on Capitol Hill and wants to reduce the power and scope of the federal government. Yet the pair has something shocking in common: despite having dramatically juxtaposed political perspectives, both Maxwell and Karoline faced opposition from leading, powerful Democrats and Republicans alike.

Maxwell's crowded primary race in the Orlando area involved a fight against nine other Democrats, including sitting State Senator Randolph Bracy and other former Florida representatives.[9] Leftist political organizers called for a withdrawal of support for the candidate after he accepted a donation from a Crypto PAC with a history of supporting pro-Israel candidates, despite his overwhelming public support for Palestinian political causes.[10] Others suggested he may be unfit to hold office because he was forced to finance a significant portion of his campaign with credit cards, tanking his credit rating and making it difficult to rent an apartment in Washington, DC.[11] Despite running with the supposed "party of youth," many Democrats repeatedly embraced opportunities to hold Maxwell's youth against him, indicating a stronger generational power divide on Capitol Hill than one between parties.

Similarly, Karoline's primary race was a difficult one in her New Hampshire hometown. Running against former Trump State Department official Matt Mowers, Karoline often found herself on the receiving end of attacks against her based primarily on age from top Republican voices. A Kevin McCarthy-affiliated super PAC known as the Congressional Leadership Fund spent nearly $2 million in the *primary* to boost Karoline's opponent and tear her down.[12] One Mowers primary ad specifically targeted Karoline as "woke, immature and irresponsible." Tell me you're worried about a new generation of conservatives stealing the spotlight without telling me, GOP. Of course, fighting against the machine paid off, and Karoline won her primary race before unfortunately losing in the general election (to everyone's surprise, based on Election Day polling).

As Gen Z continues to grow up and embrace the call to lead, it's becoming increasingly apparent that those leading the overwhelmingly Divided States of America through the two major political parties are obsessed with retaining power, no matter what the consequences may be. Perhaps today's divide is far less about partisanship than we believed, though, and indicates a generational divide that's much more frightening. If we are to truly heed the foreshadowed warnings of our Founders, I believe that it starts with acknowledging this growing divide and encouraging politically independent thought—or at least, an opportunity for a new generation of leadership in the midst of those who have held on to power for far too long.

Republicans and Democrats may retain the majority of political power indefinitely in American politics. There may never be a multitude of parties to choose from that best represents every opinion we each hold, and having a majority of independent voters may not continue beyond our generation. One thing is for sure—the two-party system has no chance of continuing to operate the way it has been with Gen Z grabbing the steering wheel.

"Finding Ourselves" without the Price Tag

I will never forget spending an afternoon in the garage with my mom at 18 years old in 2015, anxiously packing the car full of school supplies and dorm room decorations as I prepared to embark upon my college experience. College had been something I'd been looking forward to for my entire life, and it had been presented as the single most quintessential cultural experience I'd ever undertake. Countless great movies I'd seen as a kid were centered around campus life, NCAA football dominated TV screens throughout high school, and my parents' favorite stories to tell were consistently from their four years of college.

Throughout my time attending a "college prep" high school, seemingly strictly designed to prepare us for the rigor of higher education and academic life and to increase our opportunities to be accepted to the most competitive schools possible, it seemed college was all my teachers talked about. We were encouraged to pursue as many academic opportunities as possible, knowing a diploma (or two, or three) was certainly the fast track to success. Beyond that obvious truth, in the midst of my honors and AP classes, my peers and teachers alike would consistently turn up their noses at the "trashy" state schools that couldn't *possibly* provide a rigorous education. Instead, as class salutatorian (by 0.01 on my GPA—still bitter, it's fine), I was expected to apply to Harvard, Stanford, Duke, or my dream school of Notre Dame. When I was wait-listed or flat-out rejected from most of the universities I applied to, I was often given a look of pity and told I should just go to the "best" school I was accepted to—despite the $250,000 price tag and imminent student debt that would haunt me for the rest of my life.

Instead, I decided to enroll at my local state school and pursue my dream of becoming a physician by studying Biomedical Sciences at Colorado State University, graduating debt-free, and saving for graduate school. A *state* school? Gasp!

What I discovered throughout my college experience, though, was that for most Gen Zers, the consistent narrative repeated to us that a four-year degree is the fast track to success is nothing but a hollow lie. We're encouraged to get a degree in anything at all—from gender and ethnic studies to creative writing—at least in order to "find ourselves" as adults while spending hundreds of thousands of dollars we don't have to do it. Then we graduate, and it turns out no one wants to hire an unskilled 22-year-old with no foundational career expertise but a head full of leftist talking points. Shocking, I know.

Unless you're pursuing a path to medical or law school, a research field in the sciences, engineering, and a small handful of other disciplines requiring an undergraduate degree, college in today's America may actually be more detrimental to your future success than helpful. Particularly since the era of Zoom University in the midst of the COVID-19 pandemic, the curtain has been pulled back on higher education. We've departed so significantly from what academia is supposed to be that it's become unrecognizable in modern society. Instead of expanding our viewpoints, challenging our perspectives, and engaging in rigorous intellectual debate, we're being indoctrinated through a factory-like system intent on ensuring we all look different, but think exactly the same. We're encouraged to pursue educational fields that don't exist in the job market, and when we can't find someone to hire us after studying underwater lesbian basket weaving, we go back to graduate school or to pursue our PhD and ultimately become angry professors. We're graduating with hundreds of thousands of dollars in debt, moving back home with Mom and Dad, and becoming more "stuck" at 22 than we were at 18.

A 2021 study conducted by the ECMC Group recently uncovered Gen Z's changing attitude toward the college experience—while 86% of our generation reported feeling pressured to pursue a four-year degree, less than half said a college degree was necessary to attain success. Only 48% shared they were likely to pursue a four-year degree at all, while 58% believe skills-based education (trade school, nursing, and STEM) makes sense in today's world.[13] While expensive college classes became glorified YouTube videos throughout remote-COVID education, university enrollment dropped 6.6% between fall 2019 and fall 2021.[14]

So, what are we doing instead? Forging our own unique pathways to success.

Since the dawn of COVID, Gen Z has flocked in droves to skilled trade programs like construction, HVAC, and automotive repair. In fact, according to NPR, enrollment has increased across the board for these programs—sometimes as high as 40%.[15] We're skipping the hefty price tag of college tuition to directly enter the workforce, pursuing hands-on experience to add to our résumés instead of theorizing about it in stuffy classrooms. We're embracing what *Entrepreneur* magazine calls "DIY Education," incorporating everything from free online courses to YouTube videos to consume the same information others are going into debt for. In fact, while 60% of Americans believe traditional education systems are failing the current generation, 59% of us believe that YouTube will become a primary learning tool.[16] When all of the information in the history of the world is available at your fingertips, it's easy to understand why replacing the price tag with a free Google search is appealing.

When we are pursuing four-year degrees, we're becoming much more pragmatic with our field of study. We'd rather invest our time, money, and effort into degrees that will create job opportunities after graduation than feel-good majors adding credibility to our social credit scores. In fact, between 2019 and 2021, the number of students pursuing liberal arts degrees dropped nearly 10%, while there has been a steady uptick over time with the number of us pursuing STEM fields.[17]

Today, education has become far less about the diploma you earn after paying hundreds of thousands of dollars to overwhelmingly leftist educators intent on programming the next generation instead of educating us. Instead, Gen Z has embraced true intellectual curiosity. We're passionate about self-education, choosing a wise career path that will support our lifestyle, or telling tuition bills to shove it in order to enter the workforce right away. While it will take much more than an enrollment decline to fundamentally change our nation's systems of higher education, perhaps Gen Z's newfound approach to education is the first step in educating Americans for success again.

Sawing the Corporate Ladder

After my first job before college working at my childhood summer camp as a counselor and backpacking guide, my first *real* internship in college was for a United States senator from Colorado. I was new to working in politics and had just started engaging in activism on my college campus, and I believed the best experience I could gain would be seeing "how the sausage was made" in the legislative branch. A few expensive trips to Ann Taylor and J.Crew and several days of orientation later, I found myself sitting at a little desk in the Fort Collins, Colorado, office for my U.S. senator taking endless calls from angry constituents and organizing office mail. Hardly glamorous—though I did learn a lot about the political process, and more so, the rigid pathway to career growth that exists within Congress.

Like many corporate career paths, if you want to work on Capitol Hill, you almost always have to start your journey as a college intern. Answering phones to record complaints from screaming people, going on coffee runs, and giving tours of the Capitol Building are the built-in precursors to being eventually hired as a legislative assistant or communications staffer making barely enough to cover rent in Washington. If you put in enough years in your member's office, you might be lucky enough to be hired as a chief of staff—then maybe, with the support of the party, you'll have a chance to run for office yourself and be elected to Congress from your own home state. *Maybe.* More likely than not, you'll retire after putting decades of your life into public service working for a handful of congressional offices with a few big wins of your career and a pension package.

The same has been said for corporate America—business majors in college are encouraged to spend their summers interning for major corporations and Fortune 500 companies with the hope their résumé will be impressive enough after graduation to be hired for an entry-level job. The moment after being hired for your first job, you're expected to give your undying loyalty to your new "work family," working late for no extra pay or answering dozens of emails on weekends in order to be considered a "team player," with the slim hope you might be considered for a menial promotion in a few years' time. Years later, you might become a manager or director of a department at your company, and if you're really lucky, someday you just might become a C-level operations officer or marketing officer before retiring. *Might.*

The prescribed pathway from college classrooms to internships, starter jobs to CEOs, student loan debt to retirement has become so ingrained in American culture that we rarely give it a second thought—despite the reality that many of the most successful people in history lack a formal education or the internship-to-CEO trajectory. Steve Jobs, Jack Dorsey, Bill Gates, and Mark Zuckerberg all became some of the world's most successful people without a business degree—or any degree at all, for that matter. Michael Dell became the youngest CEO on the Fortune 500 list in 1992 after starting Dell as a 19-year-old premed student. Dropping out of Kalamazoo College, Ty Warner became a billionaire after his Beanie Babies defined the 1990s. John P. Mackey's Whole Foods Market has transformed the food industry without a college diploma on his wall.[18]

There are literally countless other examples, all of which have captivated the dreamer generation. Rather than climbing each rung of the corporate ladder step-by-step from intern to CEO, Gen Z is throwing out the ladder entirely. Our generation is analyzing the shortcomings of the American workforce in real time and is maximizing our opportunities on day one of our careers by innovating, ideating, and creating.

Today, 62% of Gen Z indicates that we already have started or intend to start our own businesses, building a name for ourselves as the most entrepreneurial generation of all time.[19] Like many of the nation's most successful CEOs, we don't believe that a college diploma is always a necessary precursor to running a thriving business—in fact, 78% of us say it's "not very necessary."[20] Utilizing our skills as digital natives, we're still creating products that fulfill people's basic needs, but are able to market them in an entirely new way. Even if we are selling ideas over products, we're kicking ass—Gen Zers working as full-time content creators across digital platforms are a fast-growing cohort of the 50+ million creators on the internet (and the 2+ million making at least six figures).[21]

Perhaps driven by our entrepreneurial spirit, our generation is changing the nature of workplace culture entirely. Rather than giving our undivided attention to one job during the nine-to-five workday, we're embracing what *Fortune* magazine calls "polyworking" in order to obtain greater financial security and work freedom through multiple jobs. Nearly half of us (48%) have numerous side hustles, often intersecting with our usage of social media.[22] Microsoft data has revealed entrepreneurs who use TikTok for their business are roughly twice as likely to have multiple side hustles than those who do not. Flexibility and financial freedom have become Gen Z's hallmark work traits. The same data found "91% of Gen Z entrepreneurs work unconventional hours [and] 81% say they work on vacation."[23]

The *Wall Street Journal* ran a story last April titled "Your Gen Z Co-Worker Is Hustling More Than You Think," highlighting the lives of several twenty-somethings in their careers defying society's definition of lazy Gen Zers. They found that though Gen Z is "barely in the workforce, they are pushing long hours, building businesses, striving for promotions—even for their more-senior co-workers' jobs. At the same time they are running into perceptions that their age cohort cares more about work-life boundaries and rejecting 'hustle' culture than scaling the career ladder."[24]

Why reject the corporate ladder? A multitude of reasons, but namely, we believe entrepreneurship will provide a stronger pathway to success than a typical corporate gig—61% of Gen Z small business owners believe we'll be able to retire faster from our own businesses than people who take on more traditional corporate jobs.[25] Americans of all ages are also seeing their side hustles pay off—today, the average side hustle is bringing an extra $5,700 home per year on top of a normal paycheck, a LendingTree survey found.[26]

Before you think it's all about a paycheck for Gen Z, think again. The Microsoft survey analyzing our generation's entrepreneurial spirit found 82% of Gen Z small business owners are prioritizing "social good," and it's helping our businesses grow. We're identifying modern needs in society and putting our drive, ideation, and heart for our communities together to innovate a stronger future that benefits us all.

Turns out, we aren't just a generation of dreamers with our heads in the clouds disillusioned by a far-off utopian impossibility—we're a generation of doers. We're kissing internships and grunt-work starter jobs good-bye and starting our careers at the top of the corporate ladder. Who knows where we'll climb from here?

Trusting People over Programming

Early on in my content creation and political commentary career, I remember feeling so many butterflies in my stomach every time I was asked to appear on national news to break down the current events of the day. Even calling in through Zoom from my house to a small news station, let alone showing up to a professional studio, felt like "making it" in the political world—a sentiment that was certainly echoed by my parents, grandparents, aunts and uncles, and family friends, who begged me to remind them every time I was on TV so they could turn it on.

Generationally, I suppose that was true; I had "made it," in a sense. As news and media continue to dramatically evolve daily in modern society, however, Gen Z has embraced a new format with infinitely more possibilities and reach than what we've considered to be "mainstream" in decades past. In the era of "fake news," outlets pushing overtly partisan agendas and rampant bias seeping from our television screens, newspapers, and magazines alike, Americans are trusting media less and less. In February 2023, *half* of the Americans surveyed in a Gallup poll shared that "they believe national news organizations *intend* to mislead, misinform or persuade the public to adopt a particular point of view through their reporting." Furthermore, 52% believe national news outlets don't have the best interests of their consumers in mind, and 55% say there is a great deal of political bias in news coverage.[27] Hard to imagine why, when we're living through one of the most polarizing times in our nation's history.

As a result, mainstream media outlets are confronting dramatic drops in their audiences. In the same month the aforementioned Gallup poll was conducted, CNN's viewership sank to a ten-year low.[28] Fox News topped viewership charts, reaching 2.2 million primetime viewers in the month of February.[29] That sounds like a huge number, until you start comparing reach with alternative media sources—namely, independent creators covering even more news stories with more relatable commentary.

In February 2023, my independent Instagram account alone (not including other platforms) reached 9.1 million unique accounts—8.8 million of whom weren't even following me to begin with. I don't say that to make myself sound like a baller (though it is pretty cool, I suppose), but to paint a picture for you of the future of content and information dissemination beyond what we've considered to be "successful" news sources and toward independent content creation. My Instagram profile is a messy, colorful hodgepodge of political and cultural commentary, trending stories in the news cycle, and adorable pictures of my corgi—and every *day* has the potential to reach the same number of unique individuals the most-viewed cable news channel reaches in a *month*.

More Gen Zers are turning to short-form content to consume commentary and breaking news alike, from Instagram Reels to YouTube Shorts and even TikTok, which boasts more than 150 *million* unique active users in the United States today (and more than 1 billion unique active users around the world).[30] Pew Research recently discovered that more than a quarter of American adults under 30 regularly consume news through TikTok.[31] Creators like me running relatively small accounts in the world of content creation have the potential to reach infinitely larger audiences than anyone previously thought possible with the simple touch of a button.

In fact, the influence of TikTok and other short-form platforms is so powerful that they've catalyzed many of today's most important cultural conversations. Representative Jeff Jackson (D-NC) is utilizing TikTok to educate Gen Z on what happens behind the scenes on Capitol Hill and break down complicated legislation to an astounding 2 million+ followers.[32] Rather than siloing himself into an audience of Democrat voters, he's intentionally creating content that will resonate with young conservatives looking for political unity in the 2020s. Chaya Raichik, more often known by her alias "Libs of TikTok," has dedicated her time to reposting some of the most truly insane content the internet has to offer—from teachers grooming kids to change their pronouns to Disney+ shows and school curriculum indoctrinating children with critical race theory. Her reposts have spurred infinite debates online and IRL and have caused her anonymous accounts to gain millions of followers and be highlighted on everything from *The Joe Rogan Experience* to Tucker Carlson's former Fox News show.[33]

Gen Z isn't just consuming short-form commentary, either (though it is a significant portion of the content we're engaging with). Today, independent creators are leveraging every platform possible to replace the endless hours of TV news with livestreaming on Twitch, YouTube, and Rumble. Former Young Turks personality-turned-Twitch-streamer Hasan Piker (a millennial) pioneered a new generational format for commentary in the gaming platform's "Just Chatting" section, where today he streams for hours daily with a focus on politics and social issues to his 2.5 million followers (who are largely Gen Zers).[34] Now one of the most prominent and recognizable faces on the platform, he's one of the highest-paid streamers on Twitch, earning nearly $3 million from August 2019 to October 2021 per a Twitch payout leak.[35]

Hasan doesn't pretend to be unbiased—to the contrary. His recent streams have focused on the abortion debate, our nation's impending banking crisis, and his belief in the need for universal health care.[36] Truly, though, his unprecedented transparency with his audience regarding his personal stances on every issue discussed yields an even greater level of trust. There is no secret, hidden agenda behind the scenes. What you see is what you get, which is a 30-year-old self-described libertarian socialist (there's a lot to unpack there) working toward a "post-capitalist" society. While we have very little to politically agree upon, I have long been fascinated by his content style and authenticity that's so obviously resonating with a Gen Z audience.

The reason I love streaming as a creator more than creating any other type of content is the authenticity. Every day, I have the privilege of sharing my thoughts on current events in real time—no script, no teleprompter, no fancy studio with thousands of dollars of fancy equipment. It's just a twenty-something in her spare bedroom at home, in her sweatpants, interacting in real time with the thousands of people watching live from all over the world in our live chat and building a tangible sense of community through our screens. It's not paid for by a big media corporation, there is no secret script hiding on my computer screen, and I am able to provide genuine commentary free of any external biases from my own point of view.

Streaming is, without a doubt, the future of content and commentary—and not just from the Left. Beyond my independent livestream providing a right-of-center voice to Gen Z, there are many others embracing a shift into authentic content in real time. Conservative media powerhouse the Daily Wire has begun investing heavily into this emerging field through promoting my friend and fellow Gen Z creator Brett Cooper with her show *The Comments Section*, which amassed a shocking 2 million YouTube subscribers in just over a single year and millions of TikTok and Instagram followers to boot.[37] Brett's youthful commentary on everything from the body positivity movement to video games garners millions of views daily across platforms and is providing a unique perspective to a generation who otherwise may never encounter a YouTuber and streamer with a conservative political perspective.

Dennis Prager's PragerU, most well known for their educational five-minute videos, has been host to *Unapologetic*, a daily livestream featuring the spunky Amala Ekpunobi. A former leftist and BLM activist-turned-outspoken conservative, Amala advertises her stream as "just hanging out and talking about trending topics" to her 1 million+ subscribers on YouTube.[38]

No longer is it necessary, either, to sign with a prominent media company or news network to create content that reaches the masses. Independent creators have endless platforms to choose from—importantly, platforms that value and protect freedom of speech in the digital age, which is so often under attack in the 2020s. YouTube competitor Rumble was founded with the mission to stand "for people with something to say and something to share, who believe in authentic expression, and want to control the value of their own creations...Because everyone benefits when we have access to more ideas, diverse opinions, and dialogue."[39] Remotely competing in the same space as YouTube or Twitch as a long-form video platform was once considered an impossible feat, but today is a reality thanks to Rumble's rapidly growing base of 71 million monthly active users and status as a publicly traded company.

Today, Rumble boasts an impressive lineup of Rumble-based creators and content featuring Russell Brand, Dave Rubin, Tulsi Gabbard, SteveWillDoIt, and more. Independent conservative commentator Steven Crowder recently signed exclusively with Rumble, and on his first day livestreaming on the platform garnered an unimaginable 120,000 live viewers (people watching in real time).[40]

It's never been more possible to make a notable difference in culture with a single push of the "post" button on digital platforms and social media, perhaps for the first time without the backing or investment of a major media company, cable television, or corporate news. Gen Z's overwhelming embrace of independent creators and social media platforms alike has catalyzed a forever shift in how information and commentary are presented. Long gone are the days of too much TV makeup, brightly lit studios, and carefully worded teleprompter scripts. Instead, we're flat out rejecting mainstream media and replacing it with independent voices we can directly resonate with and relate to—which we trust infinitely more.

Putting Our Money Where Our Mouths Are

It may come as a shock to discover that, despite our young age, Gen Z is fundamentally redefining consumerism today. In 2020, we already made up 40% of the American consumer base (a figure that's only ballooned since then), and by 2026, we are poised to outgrow millennials as the largest consumer base in the country, according to NCR.[41] As the soon-to-be majority of consumers, Gen Z's influence is driving a shift in marketing, product development, and more that's starkly at odds with how we've done things in the past.

Like the businesses we start and the digital content we interact with, we're looking for one hallmark trait above all else in the products we purchase and companies we pay: authenticity. The NCR Corporation believes companies should plan ahead to pass Gen Z's smell test—as it's not as easy as you might think. In 2020, they shared on their website, "They want relatability, all the way from the ads they see to the person behind the cash register. Not to mention, their hunger for authenticity compounds during times of social or political unrest. Gen Z consumers want to know the brands they support and also support the causes they care about, and if they don't, they have no problem taking their business elsewhere."

Like most Gen Zers, I've made countless consumer decisions to make the switch away from companies that, let's face it, hate me and have disdain for my values. After Ulta hosted a podcast featuring two trans content creators sharing their desire as biological men to become mothers someday and representing the face of girlhood, I made the choice to never go back.[42] To this day, I haven't set foot inside an Ulta store and have purchased new, nontoxic makeup and skincare online directly from the manufacturer. I go out of my way to purchase products from companies that create their products in America, support conservative values, and conduct ethical business practices, and I have no problem ditching those companies I've spent years financially supporting if they'd rather cater to the woke mob than create a good product worthy of purchasing.

Truly, the fastest way to lose the attention of a Gen Zer is through advertising that feels too forced, fake, and hypermarketed. Remember what happened with Anheuser-Busch's decision to feature trans content creator Dylan Mulvaney on cans of Bud Light?[43] The company's effort to cater to the Left's message of the day resulted in the almost immediate loss of $5 billion+ in market value within days. Why anyone would drink "beer" that tastes like warm bath water in the first place, I'm not sure, but point made.

In lieu of more traditional hypermarketing, brands have been forced to adapt to a TikTok culture valuing relatability and cultural trends over perfectly edited Instagram feeds, and those that have effectively pivoted are reaping huge rewards. Language learning app Duolingo, for example, revolutionized youth-oriented marketing utilizing none other than TikTok as a launchpad. In a span of less than five months, Duolingo grew their TikTok follower base by more than forty times and created a new model for social media culture. Suddenly, an app that's been in development since 2009 was not a new-age Rosetta Stone, but everyone's favorite account to follow.[44] Under the leadership of the brand's global social media manager, Zaria Parvez, the company's marketing shifted away from promotional posts about language learning and toward memes, snarky satire about celebrities, and dancing in the owl mascot costume. Importantly, the Duolingo account has developed a personality-brand, commenting on other accounts that have nothing to do with language learning as if they were your friend. In 2023, Zaria was named to Forbes 30 Under 30 List for Social Media—as she should be, after influencing countless other brands to follow suit.[45]

Gen Zers are nothing if not intentional, including with how we spend our dollars. We prefer to support small businesses in our communities, want the companies we support to demonstrate authentic care about the world around us, and thoroughly research the businesses we buy from on social media before making a purchase. In fact, 75% of us will do research to see if a company is being honest when taking a stand on social and political issues, instead of just gaslighting their target demographic, according to a 2019 Porter Novelli/Cone study.[46] Moreover, a company's digital presence and specific content have become even more important when you consider a newfound reality that two-thirds of Gen Z shoppers want to make purchases directly through social media.[47]

How we market products inevitably influences how we market ideas, and nothing has become more apparent than the reality that Gen Z is hungry for a change. We're throwing out the glossy, airbrushed, hyperedited marketing style of millennials and are yearning for a return to reality in every aspect of our lives, from a meaningful educational experience to our careers. Everything from the content we engage with online to the products we choose to purchase is an intentional decision, and blindly relying on youthful ignorance is a strategy that's sure to be a death sentence to anyone who refuses to adapt.

As many in power lament the trajectory of our country and long for the "good ol' days" of decades past, Gen Z has our eyes fixed on the future. Truly, reality has so fundamentally changed throughout our young lives that I believe it's an impossible feat to backtrack to the way things have always been done. Instead, a unique opportunity has been presented with our fiercely independent and headstrong generation: to embrace traditional values in a whole new way.

Gen Z's unique cultural identity is becoming a flashing marquee sign for the values that made Western civilization thrive—from our intellectual curiosity to our innovative entrepreneurism, neither of which are satiated by modern America's educational and corporate institutions. Our overwhelming support of individual independent media voices over broadcast news demonstrates our distrust of cultural institutions that have strategically harmed American culture for far too long. Our instinctual gravitation toward authenticity and reality in the midst of everyone trying to "sell us" something indicates a generation hungry for the truth and tired of culture's lies.

As the wheels of culture continue to spiral into madness, perhaps the best solution to end the cycle isn't to back up in reverse, but to break the wheel entirely. Our generation's story might not look like the white picket fence, classic car, gingham dresses, and suspenders archetype of America's "good ol' days," but our growing embrace of traditional values with a modern twist may just be what saves America from collapse.

CHAPTER 6

the great divide

In March 2023, congressional lawmakers held a hearing with the House Committee on Energy and Commerce to question TikTok CEO Shou Zi Chew over data security concerns circulating in American media for the prior several months. To say the hearing was a major flop would be the understatement of a lifetime: it was, in the kindest words possible, a dumpster fire. I wish I was being hyperbolic.

Let's rewind: an entire year before the hearing, the *Washington Post* reported that Meta (parent company to Facebook and Instagram) had contracted with a well-known conservative consulting firm, Targeted Victory, to "orchestrate a nationwide campaign seeking to turn the public against TikTok." How would such a feat be accomplished? Placing op-eds and letters to the editor in various news outlets and pushing politicians to take down Meta's biggest competitor in the social media space. Internal emails from the consulting firm shared with the *Post* demonstrate that employees were instructed to portray TikTok as "owned by the Beijing-based company ByteDance, as a danger to American children and society," all while detracting from public opinion turning against Meta at the time. Even more alarming: firm staffers were specifically encouraged to deflect from Meta's own data privacy and antitrust concerns by pegging the same concerns on TikTok.[1]

Why turn public opinion against TikTok? It's not hard to understand why: the once unrivaled social media giant Meta is falling behind with Gen Z. Their own internal research has found teens are spending two to three times more time on Tik-Tok than on Instagram, and it's no secret that Facebook is no longer a youth-centric platform.[2] Today, there are more than 150 million Americans on TikTok, as NBC reported, and 60% of the app's users are Gen Zers, according to *Forbes*.[3] Despite Meta's massive influence over culture, it's clear they're failing to keep up with TikTok's allure for what's soon to be America's largest single consumer base—my generation.

Okay, fast forward: after a year of meticulously placed op-eds, primetime news stories, and lobbying campaigns, the House of Representatives called a hearing to determine whether TikTok truly presented a danger to American society once and for all. Unsurprisingly, though, members of the committee weren't actually interested in getting answers to their multitude of questions concerning data privacy, the app's content, or national security. Instead, the hearing quickly became political theater, grandstanding before the American people from the high ground of supposed moral superiority on Capitol Hill.

It instantly became obvious that despite having the supposed authority to *regulate* the internet, not one congressional representative really *understood* the internet. In real time throughout the hearing, clips began circulating on (ironically) TikTok that revealed the complete lack of social media awareness held by those seeking to regulate it. Representative Buddy Carter, a Republican from Georgia, engaged in a bizarre line of questioning related to the app's ability to locate your eyes when using facial features, like wearing a fake pair of sunglasses.[4] When Shou Zi Chew simply explained this ability is not operating in perpetuity, but only when using face filters, Representative Carter asked why the app doesn't track the dilation of someone's pupils or use facial recognition to know how old their users are. Chew was tasked with informing the congressman that the age of TikTok's users is determined by the age provided when you make an account and verifying it through the public videos they post on the platform. Of course, almost immediately, Representative Carter said tracking the *public videos* of TikTok's users was unacceptable, saying, "Well, that's creepy, tell me more about that!"

Representative Kat Cammack, a Republican from Florida, identified a video threatening members of the committee with an animated firearm—clearly a violation of TikTok's community guidelines—that had not been removed after forty-one days on the platform. She said, "Your own community guidelines state that you have a 'firm stance against enabling violence on or off TikTok...When there is a threat to public safety or an account is used to promote or glorify off-platform violence, we ban the account.' This video has been up for forty-one days. It is a direct threat to the chairwoman of this committee, the people in this room, and yet it still remains on the platform, and you expect us to believe that you are capable of maintaining the data security, privacy, and security of 150 million Americans where you can't even protect the people in this room?"[5] Of course, on a platform of more than 1 billion users around the world and countless billions of videos, there are certain to be a few that violate community guidelines which fall between the cracks. Insinuating that a single video threatening congressional members with an animated firearm warrants the banning of an entire platform, however, demonstrates how little these members understand the threatening behavior on the internet in totality. I cannot begin to tell you how many death threats, threats of violence, and hateful comments and messages I've received—not *once* through Tik-Tok, but regularly through Twitter, Instagram, and Facebook.

Perhaps most egregiously (and most memed on TikTok) was a question from Representative Richard Hudson, a Republican from North Carolina, concerning the app's security: "Mr. Chew, does TikTok access the home Wi-Fi network?"[6]

Watching this clip in particular, I found my brain asking itself, "I'm sorry, did a member of Congress just ask if an app on your phone requiring internet connectivity connects to...the internet?"

I credit Mr. Chew immensely for not laughing at the congressman's question when he simply replied, "Only if the user turns on the Wi-Fi."

How is it possible that a group of powerful people *literally running our country* feel emboldened enough to regulate the platforms my generation spends hours on daily, without even understanding how Wi-Fi connectivity works?

New rule: if you don't know what Wi-Fi is, you shouldn't be allowed to regulate the internet. Everybody on board?

Through many of the committee's questions, it became instantly apparent that the information sitting right in front of each representative clearly came from a lobbying group—given that the same problems clearly exist on *every* social media platform and are not unique to TikTok. Representative Diana DeGette, a Democrat from Colorado, used an example of medical misinformation found on the platform to suggest it was TikTok endorsing this misinformation, instead of an individual sharing it. She said, "TikTok had a hydroxychloroquine tutorial on how to fabricate this from grapefruit. Now, there's two problems with that: number one, hydroxychloroquine is not effective in treating COVID, so that's one issue. The second issue is, you can't even make hydroxychloroquine from grapefruit."[7] No shit, you can't make a pharmaceutical drug from citrus.

Never mind, of course, that medical misinformation is found daily on every other social media platform, and that the same medical treatments that would get you banned on Twitter, YouTube, or Facebook in 2020 are slowly coming to light as effective in mainstream media and on social media platforms today, a few years later.

As the hearing went on, of course, some congressmen simply began saying the quiet part out loud.

Before starting his line of questioning, Representative Dan Crenshaw, a Republican from Texas, stated, "I just want to say this to all the teenagers out there, and the TikTok influencers who think we're just old and out of touch and don't know what we're talking about, trying to take away your favorite app: you may not care that your data is being accessed now, but it will be one day when you do care about it. Here's the real problem: with data comes power. They can choose what you see and how you see it. They can make you believe things that are not true...the long term goal of the Chinese Communist Party is the demise of the American power, and that starts with our youth."[8] A pretty damning case against TikTok's owner, ByteDance—but what was conveniently not mentioned was Crenshaw's alleged personal stock investments in $META, which jumped 51% in the midst of a possible TikTok ban, according to Congress watchdog website Capitol Trades.[9] Something tells me a TikTok ban would be awfully beneficial to Meta stockholders, but maybe that's just my financial illiteracy as a Gen Zer talking.

Representative Greg Pence, a Republican from Indiana, even went so far as to ask Mr. Chew, "When am I gonna get paid for the data you're getting from my children, my grandchildren?" leading many to wonder if there may be more to the story behind his bizarre question.

I could literally write an entire book about the wild saga of the House Committee on Energy and Commerce's hearing to ban TikTok—who knows, by the time you're reading these words, TikTok may be illegal in the United States. We can debate the merits of banning any social media platform all day long, which I encourage and in fact regularly participate in through my social media content and livestreams, but I don't remind you of this hearing to make a statement on the platform in particular. Though, just for fun, I should give you some food for thought: when Congress can't agree on a budget, how to secure our borders, what school curriculum should look like, or even what the definition of a woman is, how is it possible that they are in near complete bipartisan agreement to ban the most popular social media app of our time, at the bequest of its largest competitor?

Rather, I share this reminder with you to highlight that last year's hearing to ban TikTok revealed the outright technological illiteracy of our nation's leadership and is the perfect illustration that we are living in two different Americas. I often hear this narrative regarding the growing partisan divide America faces—that those on the right and those on the left are living in two different worlds. In truth, our divide between two realities is not based on partisan disagreement, but a generational disconnect.

What's playing out before us in 2024 America is a widening disassociation between America's first generation of digital natives with our fierce independence and those who came before us, convinced we're systematically destroying our nation. Baby boomers and Gen Xers spend hours on end bemoaning Gen Z's cultural impact and arguing over our role in society on Twitter threads and Facebook feeds, while we aren't even on Twitter and Facebook at all. An overwhelmingly powerful narrative has been spun condemning Gen Z as a burden on society and a stain on this chapter of American history, with very few of our predecessors willing to break their own echo chambers in an effort to facilitate generational conversation.

It's not hard to understand why this dialogue may feel intimidating to both Gen Zers and our predecessors alike. Like any time in human history, each generation has its own unique identity, characterized by diverse values and cultural norms that inform and shape our worldviews and expectations. For those who came before us, Gen Z's intimate integration with technology and social media, our departure from the rigidity of the two major political parties, and our entrepreneurial spirit over the corporate ladder all represent a significant departure from the cultural norms of their teenage and young adult years. Even how we dress, what music we listen to, and our forms of expression in the digital age are often viewed as an exodus from the values that those older than us grew up with, which I'm sure is often viewed as a cultural threat and the precipice into steep societal decline. As we already know, this isn't a new phenomenon—generational differences have been the source of conflict and tension throughout all of human history. In an increasingly complicated world, however, generational dialogue has never been more important to holding together our Western society and, frankly, life and reality as we know it.

Those seeking the destruction of this experiment we call the United States of America are hell-bent on instituting as much chaos and division as possible, allowing for the institution of totalitarianism, authoritarianism, and even all-out communism. In the last few years, we've observed a steady decline into cultural dissolution—daily observing societal disunion between Americans of different political identities, races, ethnicities, genders, and of course, generations. The widening canyon of isolation between all of us is threatening our most basic liberties and, even more important, our humanity in its entirety.

In fact, it is this overwhelming societal division pulling us apart that is leaving room for bad actors to commit acts of violence and human rights atrocities in the name of progress to begin with—ironically causing mass regression in our supposedly "forward-thinking" society. Viewing preborn babies as parasites, we allow genocide through the abortion industry to run rampant in America today. Viewing white Americans as a unilateral group of violent racists, and black Americans as a unilateral group of oppressed victims, we stir conflict in the hearts of all of us, resulting in "mostly peaceful" violent riots that wreak havoc on our inner cities and promote further racial division. Viewing biological gender as an outdated social construct holding back supposed progress, we've allowed for the surgical and chemical castration of children who struggle with their gender identity in a society that rejects gender in its entirety, rendering them infertile and likely to experience anxiety, depression, and suicidal thinking for the rest of their lives. Viewing every person who votes differently than we do as "demonic" or "evil," which sadly I hear far too often in the political world, we open the door for voter insecurity and a rightful lack of trust in our elections—not to mention, a level of partisan polarization that likely will never be overcome. Viewing younger generations as stupid, lazy, uneducated, or even malicious isolates the next generation of leaders from opportunities to grow and learn while taking up the mantle of this great American experiment of freedom that President Ronald Reagan once said is "never more than one generation away from extinction."[10]

Extinction. Not a temporary disappearance, an evolution into something else, or something able to be recovered, but an annihilation of everything we know. A permanent destruction of liberty, of justice, and *true* progress that has led the world through generations past.

I hope it's obvious that the need to bridge this great divide through cross-generational dialogue has never been more apparent. It was another great American president, Abraham Lincoln, who famously shared upon receiving the nomination to become a senator for the Illinois Republican Party his belief that "a house divided against itself cannot stand."[11] What then was a statement referencing the divide between slaves and free men today can be used to characterize any of the divisions shared here in this chapter—including our nation's many generations.

America cannot even hope to stand, to carry forward the torch of liberty into every generation to come, if those who came before us continue to shut Gen Z out of the national conversation. If we hope to hold on to any hope in bringing America into the future, we must learn how to promote cross-generational dialogue and learn from one another, giving a pathway to leadership for America's next great generation.

Each generation has, in a way, their own language through which we communicate our collective and individual values that lives on different platforms and is shared through unique means. What works for baby boomers and Gen Xers to share information—cable news networks, Facebook groups, and email chains—isn't what works for America's teenagers and young adults. Gen Zers dialogue through an entirely different mechanism, and while it's not necessary for every older American to create a TikTok account this very second, there is something to be said for being willing to go where culture is and communicate in a language that works.

As a Gen Z content creator myself, I make the conscious choice every day to bring a different perspective to our generation's favorite social media platforms—even when I am the minority viewpoint sharing my opinion. While advocating for traditional values and objective truth doesn't always yield millions of followers or virality in views (and, instead, often gets me targeted for so-called hate speech simply for challenging the narrative), I have come to understand that if people like me are unwilling to engage in dialogue with those I disagree with, our peers will perhaps never be exposed to a new way of thinking at all.

I'm tired of hearing from members of Congress or key political players decades older than myself that social media platforms—namely TikTok—are cesspools of immoral, woke content when those rooted in truth are unwilling to bring truth to those who need it most. Gen Z is lectured to by our predecessors for embracing a left-of-center perspective on the world, but it is overwhelmingly the Left who fills our TikTok For You Pages and Instagram Feeds. Not only is this targeted campaign influencing the overall cultural narrative, but it is encouraging and uplifting my generation in a way that conservatism far too often fails to accomplish.

Make no mistake about it—the American Right's disdain for Gen Z's political viewpoints and venues of communication is directly harming their chance to win. Period. With Gen Z on the cusp of becoming America's largest single voter block, the most impactful base of the American consumer market, and coming of age to run for office ourselves, disenfranchising America's youth today will spell the end of conservative values as we know it tomorrow. That sounds so *dramatic*, I know—but if there's one group that understands this, it's the Left, and they'll do anything they can to manipulate my generation through false promises and empowerment to grip cultural power with all their might.

President Donald Trump shook the political world when he began tweeting directly from his @realdonaldtrump Twitter account, furiously typing in all caps to highlight his job frustrations and general musings about culture. For years, establishment political figures and media talking heads condemned this direct pathway to converse with the American people, calling it unrefined, brash, and even offensive. I'll never forget hearing every older adult in my life, from the news anchors on television to my own parents and grandparents, groan every time Trump's brazen and cheeky tweets rattled the internet. The social media method, they argued, wasn't professional enough to be presidential. It wasn't polished enough to properly represent the Oval Office. The very idea that the president of the United States could have the capacity to successfully maneuver around traditional media was unprecedented, and no one quite knew what to make of it.

As a first-time voter in 2016, I, for one, *loved* Trump's Twitter account—even though Twitter is undoubtedly my least favorite social media platform and where I genuinely believe dreams go to die. Ha. Throughout Trump's presidency, it became clear to my generation that we didn't need to sit through hours of television programming, read boring news headlines, or watch C-SPAN to know what was happening in government and politics. More often than not, a funny tweet or even a meme could convey the same information through a more direct method, without causing us to wonder what agenda might be hidden behind the teleprompters. Trump's White House, in many ways, reinvented social media as a tool for political communication and sharing information. Beyond sharing silly Instagram pictures with your friends and family—always with the Valencia filter, duh—or friending long-lost summer camp buddies on Facebook, social media platforms effectively replaced the relevance and need for traditional media entirely.

Trump's administration began working with dozens of influencers and content creators nationwide to directly share what was happening inside the White House with the American people through expertly crafted tweets, Instagram Reels, and YouTube videos. Eventually, they even held the first White House Social Media Summit in 2019, hosting 200+ conservative creators on Pennsylvania Avenue to discuss the importance of independent journalism in the era of "fake news" and the need to protect freedom of speech in the digital age. Pictures popped up across social media of the White House decorated with posters of memes and Trump tweets, and the mainstream media had an absolute meltdown.[12] *Vanity Fair* called the Summit a "Far-Right Troll Convention," echoed by Vox, who ran a story titled "Donald Trump's Bogus White House Social Media Summit Is Basically a Big Troll."[13]

As the COVID pandemic emerged in 2020, social media again became an effective tool for the White House to communicate its response strategy and continued messaging on policy as the American people remained glued to our screens. By the end of Trump's presidency in early 2021, independent content creators like myself had begun a new journey beyond making silly videos and garnering brand sponsorships—we had essentially replaced cable television as America's go-to source for breaking news of the day, commentary, and political analysis in the 2020s.

Trump's departure from the White House following the 2020 election in the midst of a pandemic transforming the world put American politics into a state of limbo. Unsure of where a Biden presidency would take us, with many lacking confidence in the election's processes and execution, Republican leadership in particular seemed to be looking into the past for answers on how to reach the American people. It's why, from my analysis, we've seen far too many leaders on the Right continue prioritizing the economy over social issues (we all know how *that* went in '22...), herald primetime television interviews instead of building social media followings, and get stuck on 280-character Tweets instead of evolving into 60-second TikTok videos.

Expecting the next generation to encounter conservative values on Twitter instead of bringing them to TikTok is perhaps the most devastating mistake the Right could make with Gen Z, even from a sheer numbers perspective: we're talking about a platform with roughly 50 million American users (Twitter) versus 150 million American users (TikTok).[14] Moreover, far too many are still communicating ideas through the methods of decades past on TV news or through carefully placed op-eds in newspapers that the next generation will never see. Many on the Right are consistently sharing talking points about fighting a culture war from perfectly lit cable television and podcast studios, while refusing to go where culture actually *is* and change minds from the inside out.

What most people forget about marketing, I believe (coming from someone with zero marketing education, lol), is that what worked in 2016 is *not* what's going to work in 2019, nor is that what's going to work in 2023. This is true for selling products, certainly, but even more so for selling *ideas*. Ultimately, shaping culture—and downstream from culture, shaping politics—is about marketing better ideas to the next generation, over and over again. We build coalitions and break them down by getting people to think critically, to apply concepts and values to their own lives, families, and communities and envision a better world together. In the 2020s, the battle to win over culture through changing minds is happening in an entirely different way than it was even in 2019, but particularly than it was in 2016. Gen Z's method of consuming ideas has fundamentally changed, and if conservatives continue to be unable to adapt in a post-Trump America, it's hardly surprising when new coalitions aren't forming in their favor.

Interestingly, while Republicans have spent the 2020s bemoaning the rise of TikTok, it's been the Biden administration hosting influencer roundtables from inside the White House on topics like school safety, the environment, and even trans identity. Agree with the content or not, this method has been instrumental in gaining direct access to an entire generation of young Americans who otherwise would not know what's happening inside the mysterious halls on Pennsylvania Avenue. Even a confused 80-year-old with a gargantuan disapproval rating and general unlikability has somehow been navigated successfully by his communications team to at least appear to be aware of how to communicate with America's next generation. Mega-viral TikTok stars like trans creator Dylan Mulvaney post clips interviewing the president that garner millions of views, shaping public opinion for an entire generation (like it or not). Albeit cringey videos of Biden dancing with the Jonas Brothers make people laugh when at times it seems conservatives take themselves too seriously. One influencer was even tasked with making a spoof video of what it's like to be a White House intern—and as a former White House intern, I can tell you it was easily the weirdest video I've ever seen—that sparked a national conversation about the White House's continued use of content creators initiated by President Trump and carried on through the Biden era.

Last spring, the White House and Democrats announced they would take content creation even more seriously, working with an "army of influencers" responsible for touting Biden's record to their combined audience of countless Americans as we gear up for the 2024 election. In particular, the party is interested in targeting Americans "who may not follow the White House or Democratic Party on social media—or who have tuned out mainstream media altogether," according to Axios.[15] From inside the White House, several staffers have been assigned to work directly with unpaid content creators across the internet, namely TikTokers. They're even considering creating a dedicated space inside the West Wing for official White House briefings, signaling that the famous Press Briefing Room may not be the only official communications venue to the American people for long. The entire strategy, Axios says, is centered around countering the massive social media following of President Donald Trump by focusing on Instagram and TikTok to rally young voters—a demographic yet to be effectively messaged to by the GOP.

The Left gets it—if you want to hold on to power, it starts with empowering the next generation to support your causes. If you want to rally their support, you must sell your ideas in a venue and language they resonate with, and today in 2024 America, that isn't happening through the punchy tweets of the Trump era. The tough truth about the deep generational divide in America is that one side is learning to overcome it faster than the other—and those seeking to kindle the enthusiasm of my generation also happen to be the ones hell-bent on destroying our way of life as we know it. Gen Z is being sold a lie on our social media feeds about what is going to build a better future—gender theory, the *1619 Project*, transactional sex, the abortion industry, and more dominate the narrative because, overwhelmingly, those pushing this agenda are the majority conversing with us at all. Of course, when only one side dominates the conversation, it's easy to make any idea look appealing and even good. Lies become truth, and truth becomes lies if genuine dialogue isn't taking place, and today, conservatives are choosing not to engage in perhaps the most important dialogue in human history. Weeks, months, and years go by far too often before the Right's leadership wakes up and asks, "How the hell did we get here?"

In reality, the only way to preserve the foundation of Western civilization is to engage with culture, right now, right where it's at. Overcoming the generational divide in America should be the primary priority of anyone who believes in truth and goodness—forget partisan political labels—if we want to retain any semblance of liberty, character, and veracity in the future. Rather than condemning young Americans for tilting slightly to the left, the Right ought to be embracing the opportunity to change our minds and engage in cultural dialogue rooted in truth. Gen Z, despite what far too many believe, is not a lost cause. We are not too far gone. We are not brainwashed, stupid, or lazy—we're simply getting only one side of the conversation.

Generational conflict and tension have been a hallmark of the human story since the dawn of humanity, and I doubt this chapter of this book will do much to end it. However, it's important to remember that, despite this growing conflict, every generation has something unique to offer. Every one of our generations is characterized by strengths and weaknesses, and I believe that enveloping Gen Z into the national conversation through giving us a seat at the table will give us the best opportunity to create a stronger future for us all.

It's time for all Americans to remember our roots as a nation, knowing even before our country was a formal country, we've leaned on the boldness of young voices speaking in truth to take us into the future. Perhaps today, in the midst of the upside-down insanity growing in chaos with each passing minute, it is a young perspective and Gen Z leadership we need more than anything else. Learning to communicate traditional ideas through a new venue is not just important to win elections, but to preserve Western civilization as we know it.

You can keep your Twitter feeds—just consider trying something new every once in a while, too.

CHAPTER 7

giving a voice to generation z

Has anyone else ever noticed that our culture's favorite books, movies, and TV shows typically portray a young hero fighting against the antagonist for liberty and freedom, while older adults sit idly by or even chastise them for taking action?

The Hunger Games narrates a powerful story of a teenage girl who overthrows an authoritarian dictatorial government in a post-democratic America. Katniss Everdeen's courageous defiance of her predecessors sparks the fury of a nation longing for freedom and basic human rights. While most in her parents' generation are too afraid of the danger sure to accompany this fight, it's a young warrior willing to stand for truth who leads the path to victory against a too-powerful regime.

Harry Potter was an infant the first time he defeated the powerful and feared Lord Voldemort. Throughout his education at Hogwarts School of Witchcraft and Wizardry, it's three children—Harry, Ron, and Hermione—who lead the front lines of the fight against the Death Eaters while most wizards and witches older than them cower in fear (including the powerful

Ministry of Magic, by the way). By the time they drop out of school during their final year, it's these teenagers who are able to defeat the greatest dark wizard of all time and restore peace to the wizarding world.

Luke Skywalker is only 19 years old in *Star Wars Episode IV: A New Hope* when he joins forces with Han Solo, Chewbacca, R2-D2, and C-3PO to defeat the evil Empire's unprecedented planet-destroying weapon, the Death Star. While the generation preceding them witnessed the downfall of the Jedi Order and the rise of the totalitarian Empire, it's the young Rebel Alliance that ultimately achieves victory over the dark side of the Force.

More recently, it's Netflix's *Stranger Things* that brilliantly portrays the war of a ragtag group of kids from Hawkins, Indiana, who bring creativity and magic to the fight against Vecna and the Upside Down. Eleven's telepathic and psychokinetic powers fighting against the forces of evil save the world from inevitable destruction—all while adults like Mike and Nancy Wheeler's dad say things like "The government would never hurt us." Yeah, right, Ted. Idiot.

HBO's adaptation of *The Last of Us* follows young heroine Ellie in the midst of a post-apocalyptic America controlled by factions of FEDRA, the totalitarian CDC-style takeover of the United States government. Twenty years after a global pandemic of cordyceps infections, one young girl holds the key to the antidote for all of humanity—having to fight her way across America through swarms of infected, FEDRA officials, and twisted evil adults trying to kill her at every step during her most formative years.

I could share with you countless other examples—but generally, you get the point: young, courageous kid/teenager fighting against the mindless sheep of their parents' generation, a corrupt government, and a culture-gone-dystopian to bring freedom and peace to those who would come next. We eat stories like this up, binge them on our television screens, and anxiously spend years on the edge of our seats for the next season in the series. (Seriously, Netflix, *where* is *Stranger Things* Season 5?!)

Incredibly, though, we still don't seem to get it. These stories feel far away and disconnected from reality, something we can escape to inside of a screen in a scripted world to tune out the noise around us. We safely assume we'll watch a happy ending gloss our screens, victory over the dystopian authoritarianism our eyes are glued to for hours on end, and count down the days until we can watch a different variation of the same story. What we're failing to realize is that we *are* living through the same upside-down, corrupt government, anti-freedom storyline in real life—and instead of empowering my generation of young heroes to save the day, those in power are chastising us for being stupid, lazy...you get the picture.

America today tells Gen Z we should sit down, be quiet, and wait our turn. That we need to bank enough "life experience" before taking a strong stance or fighting against corruption. That we couldn't possibly have a compelling perspective in the future trajectory of our culture. No matter how many billions of dollars the entertainment industry pours into telling these stories, the message hasn't resonated with our society: the world needs young voices fighting for truth to bring freedom into the next generation. We always have, and always will.

As we know, it was young patriots speaking truth to power in the aging British monarchy that led to the world-defining Revolutionary War and establishment of the United States. Think even bigger than United States history—the epic stories of young people changing the world have existed since the dawn of humanity. It was young fishermen and tax collectors who followed the Son of God through his ministry on earth to establish Christianity, fighting against the aging Sanhedrin and Pharisees to fulfill Jewish prophecy two thousand years ago in Israel. It was even a young teenager, David, who fought and slayed the renowned Philistine giant, Goliath, in the eleventh century BC.

Just like our favorite Hollywood scripts and the stories between the pages of our history books, our decaying and regressive modern culture requires young people to fight for truth. Our generational battle may be a bit more nuanced than a scrawny teenage David slaying Goliath, but it remains just as important for our legacy and the trajectory of humanity. Today, we require the exuberance, passion, and empathy of Gen Z to bring America back to a place we are proud to call home again.

The methods through which humanity is exchanging ideas and communicating our path forward in 2024 America are not the same as decades (or even years) past. While technology and innovation continue to zoom forward (no pun intended) at a near-incomprehensible pace, it is my generation that is adapting the fastest and has the most direct experience for how to proceed. It may sound crazy to some, but 2024 America needs a generation of TikTokers, defiant entrepreneurs, and young students to chart our national course into an unpredictable future.

Our current chapter of American history, I believe, is not one we are likely to look back on fondly. Today, our nation is plagued by the lies of post-modern authoritarianism. Many cower in fear over cancel culture's silencing of dissent. Parents worry whether their children will be exposed to pornographic material in elementary school. Kids are preyed on and taken advantage of by malicious influencers online—and even by teachers hell-bent on normalizing a radical gender fluid culture. So-called peaceful protests rage on throughout America's inner cities, threatening the safety of all who live nearby. The FBI is infiltrating churches to alienate religious Americans as "domestic extremists." We're basically bankrupt (*shocker*), with no financial hope for the future of public programs like Medicaid and Social Security, let alone financial stability for our public institutions. We're culturally more divided than perhaps ever before, and the loudest voices for either political party don't seem to be doing anything to help that from the bubble of Washington, DC.

Essentially, we're aboard a high-speed train on a race to the bottom, ironically regressing our society in every way possible while slapping a shiny "progressive" label on everything we think, say, and do.

If it's not already incredibly obvious, it's time for a change. America desperately needs it. Whoever you are, reading these words, I'm sure you need it, too. We can't keep barreling down these cultural tracks and still expect to come out for the better when the train finally stops. We're at a crossroads today. How we decide to go forward will determine the future (or lack thereof) of liberty, sanity, and sadly, reality itself.

While today's loudest voices attempt to drown out any voice of hope, I believe that we need an idealistic generation of dreamers to remind us of what we should be hopeful for. To cite a powerful statistic from earlier in this book, 75% of Gen Zers in America today genuinely believe we will change the world—for the better. That's an incomprehensibly powerful figure, particularly during a time where we would probably consider our society to be at our most divided. I, too, often hear from older Americans a complete lack of hope for our country's future, convinced we've ventured too far into insanity to possibly dream of reality again. Gen Z's existing defiance of today's cultural norms is reason to have hope enough, but I'm optimistic that we have much more of an impact yet to make.

It's time for our young voices to drown out the noise and resonate with truth. It's time for us to lead the charge into the future. It's time for us to take our stand.

That might sound ambiguous, I know. What does embracing a call to speak out against culture even look like? How on earth can the average teenager or twenty-something compete with the power and resources of those older than us, particularly those in power?

If you are a Gen Zer reading this, your mind is likely emphasizing the infinite ways making widespread cultural change is impossible. Believe me, I've been there. I still *am* there, to be honest with you. It's so easy to hear nothing but the voice in the back of your head: How can I inspire others when I don't feel inspiring myself? How can I influence others without a massive following, a blue checkmark, or the opportunity to be featured on national television? How can I speak out against my insane professor and not risk failing school? How can I dare to counter the narrative without losing my friends or being canceled online? How can I change the world, when I'm far too often told I can't even change myself—that our generation is nothing but a lost cause, written off before we've even begun to write our own story?

Tune it out. All of it—the good news is, Gen Z is already making waves in changing culture. Countless members of our generation aren't waiting for permission to lead, through inspiring our peers on social media, engaging in grassroots activism, and even running for office ourselves. All we have to do to cement lasting impact is join in, taking advantage of the tools already at our disposal to fight for a stronger future.

Today's Public Square

The phrase "public square" has always been a bit of an enigma to me. Our generation's technology-driven society constantly innovating the next big website, social platform, or app has always been more of a cultural hub than an arbitrary physical location in the center of town, I suppose. Throughout history, though, it's been the literal public square in the hub of a community where culture's biggest decisions have taken place following rigorous intellectual and philosophical debate. Our freedom to express different opinions and challenge the mainstream narrative was protected in this special place, encouraging cultural battles to bring us forward into a stronger future.

Today's public square isn't so familiar or well defined. It exists through screens, in comments sections and DMs on our

For You pages and feeds on social media. It's here, rather than out in the physical world, where hearts and minds are changing. And it's here, through the venue of social media, we must be most vocal if we're serious about winning America's culture war. After all, how can we remotely expect to win over culture if we aren't willing to go where culture *is*?

Social media is condemned and attacked by many right-of-center voices and organizations for being leftist propaganda machines. While algorithms certainly are known to punish content that goes against the cultural grain, social media in and of itself is not a vice. At its core, it's a tool, a venue of communication that can convey good or bad—depending on who is willing to wield it. I, for one, am tired of being told social media is evil when I encounter countless stories of changed minds every day.

Reading this today, you may be one of those people who confronted a new perspective, opinion, or approach to an issue through social media you may have never heard before. In our culture, overwhelmingly steered by the radical Left, it's hardly surprising to me these days when I hear people say that watching one of my videos or debating in a comments section was the first time they'd been exposed to traditional values. I take my role as a content creator very seriously: I have an opportunity not only to counter the mainstream narrative, but to change the entire trajectory of someone's life by exposing them to a new way of thinking.

In fact, that's why I got started as a creator in the first place—my heart for dialogue and changing minds grew exponentially through my experience in campus activism, and I knew after graduation I wanted to continue doing the same work in an even bigger arena on social media. Telling my parents I no longer wanted to attend medical school but instead make videos on social media sure was a fun conversation, but I've fallen in love with digital activism and storytelling with each passing day since.

I got my start in content creation just after college graduation in 2019 through my first job with PragerU in Los Angeles. I had just toggled my Instagram account from private to public, had never studied marketing or graphic design, and had absolutely no understanding of what it meant to build an audience on social media. If I remember correctly, I had about 600 followers on Instagram and no following whatsoever anywhere else. At the time, my content was made up of cute pictures from college football tailgates and carousels of trips to our national parks. If you had told me then that today I'd be reaching millions of people daily across platforms, host daily independent livestreams, or have a blue checkmark, I'd have laughed in your face. Fortunately, I discovered along the way, *no one* knows what they're doing when they start posting on social media. The world of content creation is quite literally "fake it 'til you make it," with no defined blueprint for success. I simply figured it out along the way, and still pinch myself to have the independence and opportunities I've worked so hard to get in the past few years.

Social media has opened more doors for meaningful conversation and changing minds than anything else in my young adult life, so it's no surprise that my biggest call to action for you reading this book is to fight this culture war on offense right where it's happening: through our screens. Long gone are the days of reality TV, cable television, and glossy magazines impacting our culture and, consequently, our values—the easiest way to impact a generation is through authentic, real dialogue on our favorite platforms. We all have a role to play in shaping our generational identity, and it's up to us to facilitate diverse opinions free from what our predecessors want us to believe.

Engaging in social media activism doesn't require a fancy, expensive studio with professional lighting and an overpriced camera. It doesn't require hosting a "show" or series with famous guests and a professionally designed logo. It doesn't even require a massive following—all it requires is *you*.

The most powerful aspect of social media today is the ability to amplify voices that may otherwise go unheard. In today's America, those voices are young patriots longing for something more meaningful than our leftist, authoritarian, post-modern culture. When the vast majority of content shared today centers around buying into gender theory, supporting Planned Parenthood, and reposting black squares, it's young conservative voices that have the biggest opportunity for impact simply by daring to be different.

Imagine, for a moment, if there were more people posting consistently on your TikTok feed about dating with intention for marriage than vulgar hookup culture. If more of us discussed the content of our character instead of the color of our skin. If more of us told the truth about the violence of the abortion industry, wanting to *actually* support women, instead of echoing into the shallow lies of Planned Parenthood. If we exposed the reality that conservatives care about environmental conservation more than socialists do, negating the horrifying Green New Deal. If more detransitioners like Chloe Cole were reposted, sharing their horrifying experiences with the lies of pediatric gender transition, than viral trans TikTok stars like Dylan Mulvaney?

Imagine if we built a better culture, simply by daring to be louder.

If you're a Gen Zer reading this, chances are good that you're already intimately familiar with social media. Instagram, TikTok, YouTube, and more are integral parts of our daily lives, providing a platform for self-expression and connection with our peers. One recent study found the average teenager today spends roughly five hours per day on social media.[1] You're no stranger to viral videos, edgy memes, and America's biggest influencers. Today, though, I encourage you to think of social media as something bigger than your favorite place to scroll: from here on out, social media platforms are the front lines of our cultural battle.

If you're a teenager or young adult tired of the lies of modern American culture, it's no longer enough to sit on the sidelines and roll your eyes at the idiots trying to sell you Tampax with influencers who are biological men. It's time to counter the narrative on offense, creating content that celebrates traditional values with a fun, Gen Z filter.

You can start by sitting in your dorm room, the passenger seat of your car, or walking to class and recording yourself for 30 to 60 seconds talking about the crazy things happening at your high school or university. Counter something your leftist teacher said in class with the truth. Speak up about the banned words on your campus or take a picture of free tampons in the men's bathroom, tagging your school's account when you post about it. Tell us the story of a bad date you had with a guy who refused to pay because of feminism, and why you'll be looking for a more masculine leader in your next boyfriend. Take a video of the litter boxes provided at your school for your classmates identifying as furries (I wish I were making *that one* up), calling out the insanity for what it is.

Encourage more people in our generation to seek more than what our broken American culture has to offer. Explain why your heart longs for marriage and family in a culture demonizing both. Articulate your passion for your faith and religious practices while surrounded by a culture of Godlessness. Stand up for your biological gender and unique masculine or feminine characteristics living in a culture trying to erase both.

With each passing day, I come across more and more Gen Zers willing to go on offense with their content—and it's working.

Look at Maya's TikTok account @liveitloudmaya, advocating for a culture of life and countering the lies of the abortion industry through selfie videos in her car or bedroom, garnering 3.5 million+ likes on an overwhelmingly pro-abortion platform. Over on Instagram, the amazing @noellefitchett is a "Gen Zer navigating politics and culture for the glory of Christ," according to her bio. Her feed is dedicated to telling her story of transformation from social justice activism to conservative values, debunking the lies of gun control, hookup culture, and gender theory along the way. My friend @benjibacker, founder of the American Conservation Coalition, has dedicated his social media to highlighting the conservative approach to environmentalism and conservation—hardly a popular stance to take online.

The hilarious @justin_awad has built a massive online community across platforms asking his peers simple man-on-the-street questions to highlight the lack of genuine education in America today. When countless Gen Zers can't answer simple questions like "What year was the War of 1812?" or even "How many eggs are in a dozen?" it's easy to expose how much the American education system has failed. And before you ask, he'll tell you himself—no, they're not staged.

@Matt_and_Abby have become one of the most recognizable couples on TikTok, amassing a following of more than 5 million people and nearly half a billion likes. Together, they share their story of getting married young, waiting until marriage to have sex, and starting a family with their baby and another on the way.

Bernadine Bluntly, a wife and mom of five kids, has created an online community countering feminist culture called @fear-less.femininity, empowering Gen Z women to reject the lies of modern feminism and embrace their God-given femininity. She regularly highlights transformation stories of Gen Zers with "before and after" pictures of their journey away from toxic feminism, and boldly tells the truth with carousel posts like her recent "You've Been Lied To," "4 Things Men Seek in a Woman," and "Why I Don't Recommend Modern Dating."

Similarly, Brendan Schmidt is empowering men in my generation to embrace their God-given manhood in a culture that has successfully vilified all things masculine. His account @masculinerevival is aimed at "Making Men, Marriage, & Family Great Again," defined in his bio, and posts focus on how to empower young men to reject modern culture and embrace leadership roles in society. His community Masculine Revival Brotherhood even goes a step further than social media posts to give young men a sense of real connection with one another, desperately needed in an isolated and depressed generation.

Changing minds, and consequently lives, doesn't require a big financial investment, a job at a major media company, connections with talent agencies, or a beautiful set—but it does require you. We each have a role to play in changing our culture by going on offense where culture is, and it starts on social media. Trust me when I say the hardest part is just getting started. You'll finesse your content, your style, and your personal brand over time the more you experiment and grow an audience—but our generational brand can't wait any longer. Today, pick up that phone and hit post. You never know who it may impact.

Take to the Streets

Though our modern public square exists in the metaverse more than America's streets, there's still something powerful about grassroots activism. In many ways, Gen Z is reigniting the role of boots-on-the-ground change in our communities. We're protesting with homemade posters, marching for causes we believe in, and reviving a physical presence in making cultural change. The most notable examples that immediately come to mind may be in support of the Left, but Gen Z's grassroots activism isn't operating in an echo chamber.

March for Our Lives quickly became one of the most successful youth-organized movements in modern America following the devastating Parkland high school shooting, which resulted in the murder of seventeen students and staff members at Marjory Stoneman Douglas High School in 2018.[2] Founded by a coalition of students in the days following this gruesome tragedy, March for Our Lives has repeatedly rallied millions of Americans to march in favor of gun control nationwide, lobbying for anti-gun candidates and legislation and successfully registering 50,000+ new voters along the way.[3] The movement even gave rise to Maxwell Frost, a former March for Our Lives activist, on his path to become the first Gen Z member of Congress. Whether you agree with their cause or not, it's an impressive undertaking, especially since it was run by a group of high schoolers.

Like the suffragist movement for women's votes, the Civil Rights Movement for equal protection under law, and the Vietnam War protests, young people taking to the streets are making a profound impact again in the 2020s. We're witnessing millions of teenagers and young adults march side by side in favor of gun control, the Green New Deal, abortion on demand, and more, but the March for Our Lives model does not have to be the standard for Gen Z activism.

Right-of-center grassroots organizations on college campuses are facilitating dialogue, hosting events, and protesting against authoritarian speech policies every day. Groups like Young Americans for Freedom, Network of Enlightened Women, and Turning Point USA are embracing boots-on-the-ground activism from a conservative point of view, and they are shaking things up. It was after starting a Turning Point USA chapter on my college campus in 2017 that I began receiving death threats, had my address doxxed, and became Antifa's favorite enemy in the state of Colorado. It was also then, however, that I was able to connect with my peers through meaningful one-on-one conversations, host in-person events with impactful speakers, and see the tangible results presenting a new perspective by handing out posters and buttons exclaiming "Socialism Sucks!" I'd later find all over campus. Years later, it's my continued work with campus-based organizations as a speaker that's facilitating some of the most impactful conversations of my career.

Beyond campus, grassroots protests and marches from a countercultural point of view are also deeply impactful. For decades, the March for Life has facilitated a gathering of thousands of young Americans on the steps of the Supreme Court demanding equal human rights for all—including the voiceless among us, preborn babies. I have attended the March for Life three times in Washington, and I am consistently blown away by the youth presence dominating the event. Overwhelmingly it's been young people steering this cultural change and fighting for an end to the atrocities of abortion, leading to the once-impossible reality of a post-*Roe* America. Youth-centered pro-life organizations like Students for Life continue hands-on activism speaking on campuses, hosting conferences and trainings to equip pro-life students to educate their peers, and even organizing local protests against state legislatures and abortion facilities. They've successfully created a path forward for the "Pro-Life Generation" in making abortion illegal and unthinkable within our generation's lifetime.

That's not to say grassroots activism is easy—unlike the comfort of hiding behind a screen and keyboard, physical protests, speaking on college campuses, and having in-person dialogues involves a level of discomfort that may seem daunting. It's easy to understand why: in today's America, daring to speak the truth in the heart of culture often leads to jeopardizing our own safety. In spring 2023, I found myself on campus with Kristan Hawkins, president of Students for Life, at Virginia Commonwealth University to deliver a speech on the lies of the abortion industry. Before we even had the opportunity to introduce our names, Antifa and radical trans protesters began attacking the event, screaming "FASCISTS AND NAZIS GO HOME," "FUCK PRO-LIFE," and countless other slogans while physically threatening Kristan and myself. Campus police were nowhere to be found—in fact, it took more than thirty minutes and the physical assault of a pro-life student in Richmond for them to show up, eventually leading to Kristan and me being escorted from the room rather than these violent protesters.

Days later, former NCAA swimmer Riley Gaines delivered remarks on the importance of protecting women in collegiate athletics at San Francisco State University after being forced to compete against controversial trans swimmer Lia Thomas. Riley's courage and leadership in this area has shocked the world: she frequently recalls being forced to undress in a locker room with a biological male, being told she deserved to win by officials but there was nothing they could do, and losing out on opportunities otherwise possible because of the NCAA's fear of backlash. The school's Turning Point USA chapter had invited Riley to share her experience and why it's important to protect and uplift women the right way—but she soon found herself in the midst of a hostage situation, being locked inside a classroom for several hours and being physically assaulted by a man wearing a dress, as Fox News reported.[4] The school's response? They were glad students angry with the "deeply traumatic" event had "peacefully" exercised their right to protest, KRON4 reported.[5] You can't make this stuff up.

A few weeks before, my friend Ian Haworth had been asked to deliver remarks at the State University of New York at Albany—but was unable to after being screamed at, threatened, and shut down from a hecklers' veto.[6] Appearing alongside me on the news about campus protests, he later said students destroyed a Bible as part of their protest in defiance of Western values based on a Judeo-Christian foundation.

We hear far too often about these stories of extreme division, anger, and even all-out violence—but I've found through first-hand experience it is through boots-on-the-ground, in-person activism I have had the most meaningful experiences in changing minds and lives. Most often, I've come to discover, you have no way of knowing how one event, one protest, or one conversation can plant seeds of change in someone else's life. Every once in a while, though, you'll get a chance to see them grow.

Just after self-publishing my first book about campus-based activism and my personal college experience, I set off on a speaking tour across America's college campuses (literally, from Hawaii to Manhattan and everywhere in between) discussing the importance of grassroots change. Given that *Frontlines* centered around my collegiate journey, it seemed only fitting that I kick off the tour at my alma mater, Colorado State University.

After delivering my speech to a crowded room of students, I sat down to sign copies of my books for those in attendance. With my head buried into a stack of Sharpies and hundreds of crisp new pages, I heard someone with an uncannily familiar voice ask me to sign their copy.

Instantly, my eyes shot up. Standing before me was a young man who I'd worked with for several years during college in our student government association (for the sake of his privacy, we'll call him John). Throughout endless weekly student Senate sessions, campus events, and hours in our office, John had previously identified me as a clear enemy to everything he believed in. While I was the outspoken conservative at CSU, confident in casting my ballot for Donald Trump in 2016 and hosting speakers like Candace Owens and Dennis Prager on campus, John was a *literal* registered Communist Party voter. I didn't even know you could do that. He believed in a mandatory government firearms buy-back program, thought the First Amendment was too broad in its acceptance of "hate speech," and genuinely sought to build an authoritarian socialistic society.

John and I could not have been more different—and boy, did it show. Our arguments often reverberated off the four walls of our Senate chamber, discussing the merits and frustrations of one another's opinions as we set out to create policy for the student body and properly manage our student fee budget. I never backed down from the opportunity to dialogue. In truth, I believed our back-and-forth was quite fun! John presented an opportunity to articulate my values in an unfriendly environment with confidence and grace, something my peers weren't often exposed to, and

I believed I could change many minds through our arguments—though never his.

The dynamic of our debates changed forever when John decided to text a mutual friend a death threat directed toward me. It seemed my hosting of Turning Point USA founder Charlie Kirk on campus for a speaking event inevitably cemented my status as a Nazi, and from John's perspective, "All Nazis deserve to be fucking shot."

For the first time, I didn't find our ideological sparring fun. I realized the consequences of speaking truth to a world rejecting it went beyond bad grades or losing friends—it may even mean losing my own safety or, God forbid, my *life*. For a few weeks, I avoided leaving my apartment, wondering if this was all worth it, before deciding to continue the work I was doing on campus as a student activist. My parents begged me to keep my head down and focus on my schoolwork instead of contesting the majority opinions of my peers, concerned for my safety. I'm sure my grandparents were clutching their rosaries, begging God to send me in any other direction than my current career trajectory—oops—but I knew this threat was going to be one of many. Besides, if I threw in the towel in speaking truth to my campus and generation at large, would anyone else feel inspired to replace me?

As you can imagine, then, I was floored to see John standing in front of me after waiting in line to purchase a copy of my book—and then get it *signed*. Somewhere in the back of my mind I remember thinking, "I sure hope you don't read this, because I published the death threat you sent me." I can still remember feeling my jaw fall open when I looked up at my former Communist classmate, but something obvious had changed in him. Gone were his pretentious outfits and the crease between his eyebrows; they'd been replaced by dusty cowboy boots, a button-down shirt, and a soft kindness in his eyes. I attempted to squeak out a "hello" before gently taking his book, but he held on to it.

John looked into my eyes and said the last thing I would have expected, "Before you sign this, I just want to tell you from the bottom of my heart how truly sorry I am." Wait, *what*?! He continued, "I genuinely had no one else in my life ever speak to me from the position of a different perspective until you did, and at the time I was defensive because I truly didn't know what I believed in. None of my family members, friends, or professors ever bothered to challenge my values, and I clearly didn't handle it very well."

At this point, I honestly felt like my soul left my body and I was just watching the situation unfold as a third person in the corner. How was any of this real?

John then said, "Thank you for continuing to speak up for your values and continue being kind even in the face of so much backlash. It was because of you I began questioning my worldview, and today I'm proud to tell you that I'm a conservative, I own several firearms, and I am a completely different person than I was just a few years ago."

WHAT?!

Like I said, you never know what seeds you're planting in someone's life by loving them enough to tell them the truth. The conversations you have today, the events you host as an activist,

175

even the signs you make for a protest could serve as the first encounter with a new perspective for any one of your peers, which could change the trajectory of their entire life. Trust me when I tell you, if I could change John's mind, no one is too far gone.

It often doesn't take years of personal relationship to profoundly impact the opinions of others, either. I engage in fascinating conversations with my peers on America's college campuses countless times every semester and have been told too many times to count that I've played a part in someone's value foundation. I don't say this to make myself sound exceptional—to the contrary. In truth, these are ordinary conversations taking place in ordinary places that have an exceptional impact on our culture. It's incredibly telling that we're encouraged to run away from ordinary dialogue, avoiding confrontation with those who think differently than us out of fear. Those in power have convinced us to circumvent dialogue to protect ourselves, but it's been this conversational avoidance that's regressed and harmed our society more than anything else in recent years. Perhaps fear of dialogue isn't stemming from genuine hurt, but the fear of those in power that don't want us to think for ourselves. It's our activism that facilitates critical thinking beyond the talking points of the loudest voices and encourages a stronger outcome.

Grassroots activism doesn't have to be tied to a national organization, involve millions of people, or even change the world—more often than not, it takes place through our daily lives by simply conversing with the people in our communities. Your role in activism could look like mine as a student activist, could include protests in Washington, or could mean involvement with a larger organization. To the contrary, it could also embody dialogue over a cup of coffee with your friends, protesting your college administration's latest leftist decision, or challenging your family to a friendly debate over Thanksgiving dinner. Regardless of which path you take to engage with those around you to fight for truth, it's imperative that you do.

Remember this: no matter how much we migrate to the digital world, there's a magic with in-person connection that inspires the hearts of others to take action. Grassroots activism, protests, and civic engagement provide a visual representation of culture's trajectory into the future. Today, that visualization largely embodies a pro-socialism, Green New Deal-esque, anti–Second Amendment, Alphabet Mafia generational identity—despite Gen Z as a whole exemplifying so much more. Our commitment as individuals to represent our values in a public, visual way presents an opportunity to take our country back from the radical Left seeking to destroy it.

Gen Z is already largely civically engaged, surprising many of our predecessors with our drive and passion. Today, it's time to implement our engagement in our own lives in any way we can, utilizing the playbook of former human rights movements to drive positive cultural change for the future. It's time to put our boots on the ground.

Bringing Truth to Power

Throughout history, we've seen young people speak truth to power, which remains an important part of Gen Z's call to action in 2024. Today, though, I believe we have an even bigger call to *bring* truth to power.

One of the great ironies of our time is politicians convincing my generation our nation was improperly founded by old, white men—*gasp!*—while our current government is quite *literally* run by old, white men (and women). President Joe Biden is the oldest ever to hold the position, inaugurated at the ripe age of 78 years old.[7] Down the street, the United States Senate is led by Senate Majority Leader Chuck Schumer—born in 1950, holding his seat in the Senate since 1999, well before most of us Gen Zers were even born.[8] Senate Minority Leader Mitch McConnell was born in 1942, and has held on to his seat in the Senate since 1985.[9] It gets better—former Speaker of the House Nancy Pelosi was born in 1940 (actually older than the attack on Pearl Harbor) and has gripped her seat in Congress since 1987.[10] Yet through their collective centuries of public service, they still have major problems only *they* can solve, warranting *another* run for office? Hmmmm.

While there's nothing inherently wrong with walking more years under your feet—it's been many elderly men and women who have led the world through difficulties, trials, and tribulations and steered us in the right direction—most of those in power today have retained their power far longer than we have been alive, for all the wrong reasons. If I know one thing to be true, power corrupts even the best of us, and I have a hard time believing these particular "public servants" embody the best of intentions for the future of America. After all, they won't even be alive much longer to see the impact of their policy decisions that will shape reality for each of us for decades to come.

Moreover, today's generational gap is astounding to the point that I often question whether the people in power have any understanding of what reality looks like for us Gen Zers in America today. We already know certain members of Congress don't know how Wi-Fi works, and I would safely venture a guess that the vast majority of members have no understanding of our school curriculum, what the content of our favorite movies and TV shows is, or how radical many in our lives have become buying into gender and critical race theory. Governance over these issues and involvement in policymaking require intimacy with them, a quality today's aging leadership severely lacks.

Gen Z's identity as the first generation of digital natives uniquely qualifies us for governance in the digital age, navigating the complexities of intellectual property, cybersecurity, data privacy, and content regulation. Our daily confrontations with gender theory on our social media feeds and campuses alike have equipped us to maneuver these policy issues far more skillfully than those on Capitol Hill who are baffled at our society's inability to define womanhood. Our recent experiences handling our broken school curriculum provides an opportunity to change—or break—the system for those who come after us, rather than leaving educational policy up to those who haven't been in school for decades. As we rent our first apartments, buy our first homes, and (begrudgingly) pay our first tax bills, it's Gen Z who is able to identify the American individual's biggest economic frustrations and ideate creative solutions. Our generational trauma from school shootings in our hometowns creates a venue for dialogue about impactful solutions to keep those after us safer than we were.

There are countless other examples, but I hope you see the point: If we want today's policies to more accurately reflect an America that we are happy to call home, we cannot rely on those who have continuously failed us to suddenly wake up and change course. We must steer the ship ourselves, which starts with putting our own names on ballots.

Of course, running for office is significantly more nuanced than deciding to do so on a whim, but Gen Z's refusal to wait for permission to take on public office has already begun setting off sparks in the political world. Beyond the national stories of Karoline and Maxwell we explored earlier on, Gen Zers nation-wide are courageously putting themselves on the ballot for state legislative positions, mayoral offices, and more to directly impact their communities—and you can, too.

A few years ago, I was invited speak at a pro-life rally in the great state of Montana (one of my personal favorites), organized by a spunky young woman named Kaitlyn Ruch. Still in high school at the time, Kaitlyn's passion for the pro-life cause inspired her to organize hundreds of teenagers across the state to gather for an evening with their favorite speakers, find community, and engage in dialogue not happening through their educational experience. When I met Kaitlyn, I was profoundly impressed with her poise and natural skill for leadership. I knew immediately she'd go on to do great things, and great they were: Kaitlyn soon became the youngest Republican nominee in state history running for the Montana House of Representatives. Her platform centered around her pro-life activism experience, and in a Democrat-run district, she shocked everyone by casting her name into the political hat.

Kaitlyn's story is inspiring and, incredibly, not as unique as you may think. Run GenZ, a nonprofit founded by Iowa state representative Joe Mitchell, seeks to mobilize conservative Gen Zers to run for office all over America.[11] Elected at 21, Joe became the youngest person ever to serve in the Iowa House, and he is sharing his experience to assist other Gen Zers with a heart for conservative values to make an impact through public office.

Run GenZ's "Rising Stars" roster boasts an impressive lineup of passionate young Americans. Claire Cory, born in 1998, serves in the North Dakota House of Representatives. Calvin Callahan, born in 1999, represents Wisconsin's thirty-fifth district in the state legislature. Braxton Mitchell, born in 2000, is one of the youngest elected officials in the country currently serving in the Montana state legislature. Hunter Larkin serves as one of the youngest mayors in history in his early twenties in Goddard, Kansas. Dozens more join them in positions across America as state legislators, county commissioners, school board members, and more.[12]

Speaking truth to power through social media and activism is essential for our continued fight for the future of American culture. *Bringing* truth to power by joining our predecessors in the halls of city hall, our state capital buildings, and Washington, DC, may mean even more. Running for office as a passionate young American is no longer just for leftists, but a call to action for us all to shape the future of our country as we desire. Let's challenge our elected officials to a higher standard on the campaign trail, on the debate stage, and in the public square—it's up to us to reclaim public service from those who have manipulated it for personal gain for far too long.

Rise Up

As we continue barreling through the 2020s, we'll continue to navigate our upside-down culture with increasing intensity. Sadly, I believe we've only just begun to discover how truthless and confusing our culture can become. It's easy to feel stuck in the quicksand of insanity that today seems to be defined by, unsure of how we can find our way forward, but I promise you this: if our generation is unwilling to fight back, we won't have anything left to fight for at all.

Our post-modern America is leading Western culture in a race to the bottom, with the loudest voices in power determined to destroy everything we know. If Gen Z refuses to lead, if we buy into the lies that we're too young to understand or lack the proper "life experience" to drive culture forward, the chaos of today will only continue to grow. We aren't watching a familiar, perfectly crafted Hollywood plot line through our screens that we can expect to conclude with a happy ending: if we want to live in an America and world we're proud of, Gen Z must rise up and create it ourselves.

CHAPTER 8

beyond life as we know it

Sixteen percent. As you already know, only 16% of Gen Zers are proud to call themselves Americans today.[1] *That's it.*

I'm not sure it's possible to overstate this statistic and its monumental significance enough. Our nation was built on the foundation of national pride, of patriotism embodying the fight of our forefathers against the totalitarianism of the British Empire. Amid every major national crisis—both world wars, natural disasters, 9/11, and more—it's been our collective sense of pride in our homeland that drove us forward. Our ability to come together as One Nation Under God, no matter our circumstances, has repeatedly set the United States apart from the world at large. For hundreds of years, we've been defined by the power of *E Pluribus Unum*: "Out of many, one." Despite our vastly different heritages, ethnicities, religions, and values, we all could find peace in this special place we call home.

Until now.

Surrounded by the noise of political pundits, news anchors, and podcast hosts prophesying the destruction of America due to

Gen Z's lack of national pride, I hope to offer a different perspective: honestly, it's hard to blame Gen Z for feeling this way.

Don't get me wrong—I was raised to be and will always be proud to be an American. I remain proud of our nation's heritage. I am proud of the wealth of opportunities I've been given growing up in the land of the free. After traveling to dozens of other countries around the world, my soul is always happy to return home to the United States, and I relish opportunities to share my American heritage with others across the globe. However, as our nation continues to descend into chaos, I think it's worth asking: at what point do we acknowledge our way of life isn't what we've always been proud of in the past? At what point do we hit the wall, and say we've had enough?

When I first began conceptualizing this book, my original title labeled Gen Z as "the end of the alphabet," followed by a quippy, "& life as we know it?" I intended to convey just how much our nation has embraced outright insanity throughout the past few years. As I completed my research and began ferociously writing these pages, I've come to realize that life as we know it may not be something to desperately cling to, after all. In truth, our nation's culture has so dramatically changed throughout the past few years that it's become unrecognizable. Not only have we begun to see lies become truth, but in many ways, we've arrived in a post-truth society.

It's hard to admit, but today's America has become a hollow shell of what we were founded to be. Our foundation of Judeo-Christian values has been replaced by Godlessness and worship of self, rather than faith in something bigger than ourselves. We've created a culture that views victimhood as virtue, while victors overcoming their circumstances are a societal vice. Our education system prioritizes political indoctrination over empowering education. Beauty standards and physical fitness have been replaced with the (ironically named) body-positive movement, glorifying morbid obesity. We label truthful words violence, while actively participating in the horrific violence of the abortion industry, sexualizing children, and empowering open borders to fuel drug trafficking. We identify regular churchgoers and parents testifying at school board meetings as domestic extremists, while calling literal rioters and violent radicals "peaceful protesters." We claim to support and uplift women but say nothing when biological men take their place in athletic competitions, influencer partnerships, and even bathrooms. We attack traditional marriage as outdated, while glorifying pornography and transactional sex as empowering. We defund the police after labeling them racist, as a group, but refuse to acknowledge the consequent rise in violent crime and homicide in our cities. We'll provide billions of dollars in free equipment to the literal Taliban but continue refusing to secure our own borders.

How far does America have to lead the world's race to the bottom before we say it's time to *end* life as we know it?

As a patriotic, conservative young American myself, I am proud of our nation's heritage and history—but I'm certainly *not* proud of who we've become, and I refuse to allow us to continue down this path. Those my age deserve better. Those younger than me deserve better. Certainly, the generations who come after us at the end of the alphabet deserve better—it's time, then, for a new beginning.

In politics, particularly from a conservative lens, I've come to find far too many are focused on going back to the "good ol' days" of American culture. Returning to a time where families were strong, faith was stronger, it was easy to afford a home and kids could play on the sidewalk without fear certainly sounds picturesque, and many in power have fixed their gaze firmly on the past to escape our dystopian present—failing to bring us forward into the future.

What many fail to understand is the white picket fence, tailored suits, and golden retriever imagery of America's past today has become more like a Norman Rockwell painting than reality. Embellished. Figurative. Not quite real. In our world of existing falsehood, with culture dominated by lies over truth, what we desperately need is an authentic path forward rather than an idealistic, fuzzy longing for the past. Not to mention, it's essentially unattainable for us to picture ourselves making good money at a corporate job, buying a beautiful new home for a reasonable price, or getting married in a marriage-less culture. I would love for us to return to the setting of the past many long for, but I genuinely believe it has faded into the pages of our history books.

Instead of listening to those older than us pine away for a bygone era, today our generation must work to paint a new picture of our idealistic future. We may not even be able to come to a generational consensus on what that ideal looks like today, but it's time to at least start asking the right questions. After all, it's easy for us to look around today in 2024 America and realize our current trajectory is only creating a culture of hopelessness.

Despite our deep ideological, political, and generational division, we can all agree: This. Is. Not. Working. Maybe our future doesn't resemble a Norman Rockwell painting, but an Instagram feed filled with many pictures encompassing our many ways to fight for our future—at least united all under the same umbrella account @America.

Gen Z's embrace of conservative values will not be the first step backward to our favorite chapters of history but will courageously take us forward against the grain of post-modern culture into a stronger future. In fact, reframing "traditional values" as a path forward instead of a longing for the past may be just what conservatives need to reach young Americans frantically searching for hope. Renewing the importance of marriage and family, embracing our biological gender, seeking opportunities for free market entrepreneurship, and more are our generation's opportunities to reclaim our future for ourselves.

It's time for us to reposition our generation on offense when fighting for American culture. Long gone are the days we can comfortably assume someone else is making the right decisions for our future as a nation—if the last few years have taught us anything, it's quite the opposite. Our predecessors leading our nation today have anything but our best interests at heart, driving us into the heart of our Godless, anxious, depressed, doomsday-mentality culture we are living in today. They even have the audacity to refuse to take ownership for their failures as they turn around and point the finger of blame at you and me, blaming us for the downfall of our great nation as they continue to torpedo our opportunities for success.

I don't share this with you to discourage you, but rather to give you hope: no longer are we beholden to the failures of those in power. Instead, *we* can chart our nation's course into a stronger future, fighting for truth and goodness for Gen Z and beyond. Across America, Gen Z is already stepping up into leadership opportunities without permission from our predecessors. We're circumventing traditional media and entertainment as independent journalists and content creators. We're starting our own businesses from scratch instead of providing undying loyalty to a major corporation. We're rejecting the rigidity of the two-party system whose politicians often fail to live up to their promises. We're ditching hookup culture and dating apps, wondering if there may be something more. We're taking to the streets to speak truth to those in power. Our natural skepticism and curiosity are threatening the lies of gender theory, CRT, and the abortion industry with each passing day.

We're tired of empty promises and lack of action from those with the capacity to effectuate change—so we're making that change ourselves. Now, in our ever-changing and increasingly complicated world, it's time for us *all* to fight on offense, in any way we can. Like the chapter in our history before our nation was even formally founded, America is relying on young rebels to fight against cultural and political norms and reclaim liberty for ourselves. Given America's position on the global stage, I would even go so far as to say our nation and world are depending on our generation's leadership now. After all, at the rate America is devolving into lunacy, if we don't stand up and fight today, we won't have anything left to fight for tomorrow.

Our nation's founding inspired the creation of democratic governments around the world, sparking the French Revolution, the rise of Britain's parliamentary system, and countless other global powers. It was a generational rebellion in 1776 against the might of the British monarchy with little to no chance of success that forever shaped the fight for liberty across the world. Young patriots fighting for freedom likely had no understanding of the impact they would have on the future of humanity, but even today continue inspiring young people to fight corrupt power with truth and a longing for liberty in every corner of the globe. Could you imagine if they had listened to their predecessors saying they lacked the necessary "life experience" to create the United States of America? Thank God they had the fortitude to tune out those doubting their ability to effectuate change.

The teenagers and young adults recognized the fallibility of their current way of life in 1776, validating the need to fight for a stronger future for those to come based on truth, virtue, and freedom. Their unprecedented courage and unlikely victory inspired the hope of every generation thereafter, catalyzing a newfound hope that any individual citizen had the capacity to better their circumstances and build a country that reflected their value. For the first time in history, ordinary citizens had the capacity to shape the world at large with lasting change, and it started with their acknowledgment for the need to end life as they knew it.

Just as our forefathers redefined the entire world, Gen Z today is again confronting the shortcomings of modern culture and discovering the need for radical change. That change isn't to reject the foundation of our nation—that's already been accomplished by our predecessors—but to return to our roots. Today, we must seek objective virtue and values in a subjective, anarchic culture void of hope for the future. Our fight does not center around rampant taxation (though, to be honest, it should) and the quartering of soldiers in our homes, but instead seeks to defy the reprobate cultural norms of our time.

Our nation's standing on the world stage has led the trajectory of humanity for centuries—since our founding. We have inspired countless human rights movements across the globe, facilitated the creation of dozens of democratic governments, and ignited the longing for freedom in virtually every other society. What America believes and acts upon inevitably influences the rest of the world, and our cultural devolution throughout my lifetime has spun the globe into chaos. Gen Z's struggle to find hope is echoed by our peers on every continent, and our need to build a stronger future transcends national borders and citizenship—whether we realize it or not. Our generation's cultural revolution is imperative not just for ourselves, but for the future of humanity the same way our forefathers' struggle against authoritarianism was.

That's not to say this battle is easy. I've had significant personal experience with the backlash of living a countercultural lifestyle and encouraging others to do the same. I've gotten the failing grades on school projects, seen lifelong friends walk out of my life, and been written up at my job for refusing to comply with the leftist agenda. I've been on the receiving end of numerous death threats, threats of rape and violence, and attacks by

Antifa and radically violent protesters. I've had relationships suffer, opportunities taken away, and social media accounts banned. There have been many occasions where I find myself surrounded by insanity and have to pause to ask myself if this fight is really all worth it.

Today, I want to encourage you to know the backlash, hatred, and isolation that often come about as a result of speaking out against our broken society is *absolutely* worth it. Far before I am ever an American, a conservative, or a content creator, I am a Christian. My ultimate purpose in this life is not to sell a ton of book copies, make viral videos, or appear on national television. Instead, it's to share the message of the Savior of the universe, Jesus Christ. Ultimately, I've come to realize that this world, and even this country, are *not* my home—heaven is, and it's my calling to make this fragmented world a bit more like the next one.

That's not an easy path to take, by any means. Today in the United States, far too often Christianity has been boiled down to a feel-good, warm, on-my-own-terms religion that fails to teach the entirety of our faith. We've made our religion easy according to the demands of the world, rather than accepting Jesus' teaching at face value that practicing our faith and sharing it with others would be impossibly difficult. Following Christ, we are not promised an abundant community of people who adore us during this lifetime. We aren't promised infinite social media followers, fame, glory, or riches. We aren't even promised everyday happiness. To the contrary—we are promised that the world would reject us, hate us, and persecute us. It was Jesus Himself who reminded His apostles in John 15:18-19, "If the world hates you, keep in mind that it hated me first. If you belonged to the world, it would love you as its own. As it is, you do not belong to the world, but I have chosen you out of the world. That is why the world hates you" (NIV).[2]

As a Christian, I am called to share the gospel with the whole world, which means I am called to speak truth into a world rejecting the very concept of objective truth. After all, I believe truth has a name—Jesus Christ is The Truth—so it's safe to assume that I will receive the hatred of the world every time I share the message of the next one. Setting foot on this journey as a content creator, speaker, author, and more seeking truth and sharing it with my peers hasn't been an easy one. Believe me, I've heard it all: Nazi Barbie, Hitler Youth captain, white supremacist, transphobe, TERF, homophobe, misogynist, pig, fascist, and every other label you could possibly imagine. While at first these terms scared me and made me question the path before me, I've come to hear them for what they are—signs that I'm going in the right direction. We aren't called to be of this world, but in it, chosen to bring truth to our peers even when it's hard.

You don't need to be a Christian yourself or even religious to see this reality play out before our eyes every day. Daring to question the narrative, utter an opposing view to those in power, or change your opinion on any one of the emotionally charged topics of the day means risking everything in modern America. Your job, your relationships, your financial security, even your safety are often put in jeopardy when you dare to seek the truth instead of blindly buying into the mainstream. It's easy to reject the call to lead, and I certainly understand why it's more appealing to keep your head down and follow the crowd.

As you ponder what role you'll play in this culture war, I want you to ask yourself this question: What am I willing to give up for the price of fitting in? My beliefs? My speech? My religion? My property? My freedom?

Similarly, what am I willing to give up for the price of truth and liberty?

Despite our hyper-partisan world, I often continue to hear people desire to abstain from these vitally important conversations because they don't consider themselves to "be political." They lack passion for debating Congress's newest legislation or what someone said on the presidential debate stage, so they feel comfortable going with the flow instead of taking on the role of an active participant. If you're one of those people, I honestly don't blame you—even I am tired of talking politics as a massive political nerd. Today, though, politics and culture have become so intimately intertwined that our refusal to get involved has emboldened countless bad actors to manipulate our system and take advantage of our apathy. Who benefits from our apathy most? Our predecessors who have desperately clung to power for longer than we've been alive—and don't plan on letting go anytime soon. In 2024 America, whether we intended for it to be this way or not, what brand of underwear you're wearing and what toothpaste you used this morning *are* making a political statement, so you're participating in shaping national politics even if you're unaware of it. You might as well take ownership of living your values.

It's often said time moves faster the older you get, but I actually believe that time is moving faster for everyone today. The 2000 to 2010 era felt infinitely longer than 2010 to 2020; 2020 to 2024 has felt like a lifetime and has packed a lifetime's worth of societal change into just four years. Technology has played a major role in our societal acceleration—the introduction of the radio and television were essentially technological miracles for their time, and for decades remained in the forefront of innovation, defining culture for boomers, Gen X, millennials, *and* Gen Z. In our generational lifetime alone, however, we've witnessed the death of television and radio with the dawn of streaming and podcasts, and in the past few years alone have watched these industries transform before our eyes. The first time I saw a video on YouTube in elementary school, at the time a poorly coded website, I remember laughing at the double rainbow guy and "Charlie bit my finger." Today, social media platforms at large have completely replaced corporate news outlets, entertainment television, business marketing, and more—all within a few years' time. Even since graduating from high school, I've witnessed social media making individual people more influential than the president of the United States. In the blink of an eye, we stopped listening to mix CDs and replaced them with iPods—today, Spotify and Apple Music reign king and the dawn of artificial intelligence is even replacing songwriting. Dating has transformed from months of courtship to a "You up?" text seeking a hookup after matching with someone on Tinder you've never met before. Like a snowball down a hill, everything has accelerated faster and faster to generate the instant-gratification society we live in today.

The same can be said for our values and way of life—what it means to be an American has accelerated downhill so quickly that we've lost the opportunity to even ask where we're going. All we can do is desperately cling on while screaming, "Stop the ride, I want to get off!" We've been so obsessed with a "progressive" culture warranting constant change without evaluating the larger societal outcome that we've become reminiscent of *Jurassic Park*'s Dr. Ian Malcolm. In the midst of all the chaos, he finally stops to reflect, "Yeah, but your scientists were so preoccupied with whether or not they could, they didn't stop to think *if* they should."

If life has transformed so dramatically so quickly throughout our lifetime, imagine how much more quickly we will lose the opportunity to fight for our futures if we refuse to take action now. The only way to stop this ride is to get off—if at all possible, at this point. We're all reeling from the dizziness of our world spinning out of control, but if we take a beat to acknowledge where we are today, we'll have the opportunity to set a course for where we want to go tomorrow.

The good news is that things have devolved into chaos at an accelerating rate throughout our lifetime, but we have the capacity to effectuate positive change just as quickly if we're daring enough to challenge the status quo.

I'm not sure anyone could have predicted that, by 2024, the most punk rock thing you could possibly do was embrace traditional values. Forget massive tattoos, scandalous outfits, and nose rings—today's countercultural lifestyles are based in tradition. To reject cultural norms today is to fall in love instead of hookup with anyone. To get married and start a family instead of making work your "family." To embrace your God-given biological gender and celebrate the differences between men and women. To practice your faith instead of rejecting religion entirely, and more. Radical extremism today was the American Dream of just a few decades past.

I recently discovered that the word "extreme" is an antonym to the word "norm." While it doesn't immediately come to mind for me, I suppose it makes sense: to counter the mainstream and defy cultural standards does mean you have to be a bit extreme and on the fringe of society. Throughout history, those daring to go against the grain have always been labeled by others in power as extremists, and while we may be shocked to discover that today's extremists are people of faith, truth seekers, and young families embracing conservative values, in reality we are a bit extreme. Attempting to maintain those values in today's society feels exhausting and isolating because it is *not* the norm, but that's not to say it couldn't become the norm again in the future.

Call *me* a radical extremist, I guess (I'm sure the FBI already does, given I'm a young, engaged, conservative Catholic), but I believe we could all use a little rebellion in our lives. As I prepare for the next chapter of my life as a young adult, entrepreneur, wife, and (hopefully!) mother of the next generation, I want to live in a country that provides the same opportunities to those who come after me as I was fortunate enough to receive growing up. I want to thrive in a nation where I'm free to speak my mind, to challenge the narrative, and have faith in something bigger than what I can see. As every American generation has longed for, I hope to build a future for my family that is stronger than generations past. I long to contribute something meaningful to our American story and serve my community for the better. I seek to find pride not just in our history, but in our present and future, and I know I'm not alone.

Gen Z is aching for change, and opportunities to lead. We all deserve to find lasting joy and fulfillment in our futures. Gen Z deserves to break free from the yoke of our current mental health crisis. We deserve to find real love, to build and raise a family, and to rediscover strong marriages. Gen Z deserves the chance to build our own new American Dream, instead of being told the American Dream is dead.

We deserve a reason to be hopeful, rejecting the lies of the Left that have redefined American culture throughout our lifetime. It's time to build a future beyond our current dystopia based in freedom, truth, and goodness. It's time to fight on offense, and it starts with each one of us embracing the call to lead. No matter where you stand today, it's time for us to write this next chapter together. As you close this book, I pray you pick up the torch to bring freedom forward.

Gen Z is at the end of the alphabet, and even at the end of life as we know it—but perhaps that's not such a bad thing after all.

acknowledgments

Writing this book would not have been possible without the support of so many people who worked tirelessly to bring truth to Generation Z and fight for the future of culture. I will be forever grateful for the support, inspiration, input, and hard work contributed by those I am lucky to have in my corner. "Thank you" sounds like such a trivial phrase—but from the bottom of my heart, I truly mean it.

To each and every one of you that picked up a copy of this book, read through it, and made it all the way to the end—thank you for being willing to open your heart and mind to a radically countercultural book. It's not easy to go against the grain either as an author or a reader, and being willing to step out of our own comfort zones and echo chambers is the only way we'll be able to continue building a country we're proud of.

To my incredible fiancé, Brock—thank you for being my best friend and biggest supporter, for the endless encouragement and read-throughs of this manuscript, for the infinite strategy sessions and "talk it out" moments we had to make this idea a reality. Thank you for everything you do to support me in my faith, my professional life, and our love of adventure. I wouldn't want to do this life with anyone else and I cannot WAIT until I see you up there at the end of the aisle.

To my family (Mom, Dad, Gaby, and Amelia)—you have always cheered me on to do the impossible and encouraged me to dream bigger. Thank you for being the best family God could have ever designed for me, for our many adventures together, and for roasting me when I need it, which I acknowledge is often.

To Tyler—thank you for randomly DMing me on Instagram asking if I'd ever want to publish another book. You've been the BEST agent and such a supportive friend, and I can't wait to see how we continue to change the hearts and minds of Gen Z through every book to come!

To the entire Fedd Agency team—thank you for the incredible amount of work you all put in to pitch this book to publishers, to market a fresh set of ideas to my generation, and to help this book see the light of day. I am so grateful for each and every one of you!

Ash—Tyler could not have matched me with a better writing coach. Thank you for your endless optimism and positivity at six o'clock in the morning, for helping me stick to our many (many!) deadlines, and for helping this book become everything it could become. I am deeply grateful for your guidance and support.

To Kathryn, Alex, and the entire team at Center Street Books and Hachette Publishing—THANK YOU, THANK YOU, THANK YOU for embracing this book with open arms and taking a chance on me for my first go-around in traditional publishing. Your heart for Gen Z and our country is so beautiful, and it's been an honor to work with Center Street to bring this important message to life as we gear up for America's fight for the future.

To all of my sweet friends who cheered me on, gave advice, and offered support throughout the writing of this manuscript—Savannah, Mitchell, Emma Kate, Katie, Maggie, Gracie, Jacqueline, and so many others—thank you for always finding ways to make me smile and getting me out of countless writer's block moments. Your input in this book was (and still is) hugely important, and I couldn't do life without all of you!

Finally, to my generation—I could not be prouder of the way we are embracing the call to leadership despite unfathomable adversity and pushback every day. We are changing the nature of America and the world as we know it every day and proving over and over again we *are* made for such a time as this. I pray this book inspired you, empowered you, and energized you to continue the fight. We are the End of the Alphabet, and we'll keep fighting like hell for an America we can be proud to call home again.

notes

Chapter 1

1. Katie Bishop, "Are Younger Generations Truly Weaker than Older Ones?" BBC Worklife, February 18, 2022, https://www.bbc.com/worklife /article/20220218-are-younger-generations-truly-weaker-than-older-ones.

2. Alison Gopnik, "Why We Look Down on Today's Kids," *Wall Street Journal*, December 6, 2019, https://www.wsj.com/articles/why-we-look-down -on-todays-kids-11575561273.

3. Lauren Strapagiel, "Gen Z Is Calling Gen X the 'Karen' Genera-tion," BuzzFeed News, June 17, 2020, https://www.buzzfeednews.com/article/ laurenstrapagiel/gen-z-is-calling-gen-x-the-karen-generation.

4. Sidnie White Crawford, updated by Joshua Aaron Alfaro, "Esther (Bible)," Jewish Women's Archive, accessed April 17, 2023, https://jwa.org/encyclopedia /article/esther-bible#:~:text=In%20the%20biblical%20book%20named,the %20Jews%20of%20the%20empire.

5. Esther 4:4, The Bible, New International Version, https://www.bible gateway.com/passage/?search=Esther+4%3A14&version=NIV.

Chapter 2

1. Samuel J. Abrams, "Are Colleges and Universities Too Liberal? What the Research Says about the Political Composition of Campuses and Campus Climate," American Enterprise Institute, October 21, 2020, https://www.aei.org /articles/are-colleges-and-universities-too-liberal-what-the-research-says -about-the-political-composition-of-campuses-and-campus-climate/.

2. Gigi de la Torre, "97% of Ivy League Political Donations Go to Democrats," The College Fix, November 3, 2022, https://www.thecollegefix .com/97-percent-of-ivy-league-political-donations-go-to-democrats/.

3.   Maxin Lott, "Harvard Faculty Backs Democrats 96% of the Time, Says School Paper," Fox News, May 2, 2016, https://www.foxnews.com/politics /harvard-faculty-backs-democrats-96-of-the-time-says-school-paper.

4.   Robert M. Schmidt, "Why Universities Must Choose One Telos: Truth or Social Justice," Heterodox Academy, November 8, 2018, https://docs.wix static.com/ugd/b0cbbd_7fd2855afcff462baeb926d125af4ba1.pdf.

5.   Sonnet Frisbie, "Gen Z Corporate Activism Is Local First," Morning Consult, January 9, 2023, https://morningconsult.com/2023/01/9/gen-z -corporate-activism-is-local-first/.

6.   Matt Fradd, "10 Shocking Stats about Teens and Pornography," Covenant Eyes, April 3, 2023, https://www.covenanteyes.com/2015/04/10/10 -shocking-stats-about-teens-and-pornography/.

7.   "Over 75% of Dating App Users Experienced Sexual Violence in Past 5 Years, Says Report," WION, October 4, 2022, https://www.wionews.com/world /over-75-of-dating-app-users-experienced-sexual-violence-in-past-5-years -says-report-522284.

8.   Kristen Bialik, "For Valentine's Day, 5 Facts about Single Americans," Pew Research Center, February 8, 2023, https://www.pewresearch.org/short -reads/2023/02/08/for-valentines-day-5-facts-about-single-americans/.

9.   Kim Parker, Juliana Horowitz, Anna Brown, Richard Fry, and D'Vera Cohn, "Dating and Relationships in the Digital Age," Pew Research Center, August 20, 2020, https://www.pewsocialtrends.org/wp-content/uploads/sites /3/2020/08/PSDT_08.20.20.dating-relationships.final_.pdf.

10. Joseph Chamie, "The End of Marriage in America," The Hill, August 17, 2021, https://thehill.com/opinion/finance/567107-the-end-of-marriage-in-america/.

11. "Divorce Statistics and Facts," Wilson & Fishman, LLC, https://www .wf-lawyers.com/divorce-statistics-and-facts/.

12. "US Birth Rate Falls 4% to Its Lowest Point Ever," BBC News, May 6, 2021, https://www.bbc.com/news/world-us-canada-57003722.

13. "Stress in America™ Generation Z," American Psychological Association, October 2018, https://www.apa.org/news/press/releases/stress/2018 /stress-gen-z.pdf.

14. "Drug Facts: High School and Youth Trends," National Institute on Drug Abuse, June 2016, https://nida.nih.gov/sites/default/files/df_high_school _and_youth_trends_june2016_final.pdf.

15. "Underage Drinking," National Institute on Alcohol Abuse and Alcoholism, March 2023, https://www.niaaa.nih.gov/publications/brochures-and-fact -sheets/underage-drinking.

16. "Sadness and Violence among Teen Girls and LGBQ Youth," Centers for Disease Control and Prevention, March 9, 2023, https://www.cdc.gov/nchh-stp/newsroom/fact-sheets/healthy-youth/sadness-and-violence-among-teen-girls-and-LGBQ-youth-factsheet.html.

17. "New Government-Funded Food Pyramid Says Lucky Charms Are Healthier than Steak," Good Ranchers, January 12, 2023, https://www.goodranchers.com/blog/new-government-funded-foodpyramid-says-lucky-charms-are-healthier-than-steak.

Chapter 3

1. Emma Chiu, "Generation Z Is on a Mission to Build a Better Normal for All," Warc, October 1, 2021, https://www.warc.com/newsandopinion/opinion/generation-z-is-on-a-mission-to-build-a-better-normal-for-all/en-gb/4013.

2. Nidhi Pandurangi, "Gen Z Is Already Changing What It Means to Live, Work, and Shop in America in Six Key Ways," Business Insider, February 27, 2023, https://www.businessinsider.com/gen-z-changing-america-shop-live-work-millennials-2023-2.

3. Todd Andrlik, "Ages of Revolution: How Old Were They on July 4, 1776?" *Journal of the American Revolution*, August 8, 2013, https://allthings liberty.com/2013/08/ages-of-revolution-how-old-1776/.

4. Roxanne Roberts, "The Senate's Retirement Wave: The Oldest and Longest-Serving Members," *Washington Post*, June 2, 2021, https://www.wash ingtonpost.com/lifestyle/2021/06/02/senate-age-term-limits/.

5. Media Insight Project, "The News Consumption Habits of 16- to 40-Year-Olds," American Press Institute, August 31, 2022, https://www.american pressinstitute.org/publications/reports/survey-research/the-news-consumption-habits-of-16-to-40-year-olds/.

6. John Burn-Murdoch, "Millennials Are Shattering the Oldest Rule in Politics," *Financial Times*, December 29, 2022, https://www.ft.com/content/c361e372-769e-45cd-a063-f5c0a7767cf4.

7. Casey Harper, "Younger Americans Identify as Independent More than Republicans, Democrats Combined," The Center Square, August 18, 2022, https://www.thecentersquare.com/national/younger-americans-identify-as-independent-more-than-republicans-democrats-combined/article_2c01b5a4-1f10-11ed-9ec9-9f2b0759a2d7.html.

8. Ashley Stahl, "Why Democrats Should Be Losing Sleep Over Generation Z," *Forbes*, August 11, 2017, https://www.forbes.com/sites/ashleystahl/2017/08/11/why-democrats-should-be-losing-sleep-over-generation-z/?sh=46aa5d447878.

9. Ashley Lopez, "Turnout among Young Voters Was the Second-Highest for a Midterm in Past 30 Years," NPR, November 10, 2022, https://www.npr .org/2022/11/10/1135810302/turnout-among-young-voters-was-the-second -highest-for-a-midterm-in-past-30-years.

10. Zachary Wolf, "Exit Polls Show How the 2022 Midterm Election Changed Since 2018," CNN, November 9, 2022, https://www.cnn.com/interactive /2022/politics/exit-polls-2022-midterm-2018-shift/.

Chapter 4

1. "Gen Z Smarter, More Skeptical than Millennial Counterparts," Retail Customer Experience, February 16, 2022, https://www.retailcustomerexperience .com/news/gen-z-smarter-more-skeptical-than-millennial-counterparts/.

2. "Gen Z Finding Meaning," EY, https://www.ey.com/en_us/consult ing/is-gen-z-the-spark-we-need-to-see-the-light-report/gen-z-finding -meaning.

3. Jeffrey M. Jones, "Millennials, Gen X Clinging to Independent Party ID," Gallup.com, May 31, 2023, https://news.gallup.com/poll/397241/millennials -gen-clinging-independent-party.aspx?utm_source=alert&utm_medium=email &utm_content=morelink&utm_campaign=syndication.

4. Filippo Menczer, "Here's Exactly How Social Media Algorithms Can Manipulate You," Big Think, October 7, 2021, https://bigthink.com/the-present /social-media-algorithms-manipulate-you/.

5. Tammy Qui, "A Psychiatrist's Perspective on Social Media Algorithms and Mental Health," Stanford Institute for Human-Centered Artificial Intelligence, September 14, 2021, https://hai.stanford.edu/news/psychiatrists-perspective -social-media-algorithms-and-mental-health.

6. Morgan Baskin, "Kamala Harris Called Young People Stupid in 2015," Vice, July 8, 2019, https://www.vicecom/en/article/qv79xq/kamala-harris-called -young-people-stupid-in-2015.

7. Erin Doherty, "The Number of LGBTQ-Identifying Adults Is Soaring," Axios, February 19, 2022, https://www.axios.com/2022/02/17/lgbtq-generation -z-gallup.

8. "On the Cusp of Adulthood and Facing an Uncertain Future: What We Know About Gen Z So Far," Pew Research Center, May 14, 2020, https://www.pew research.org/social-trends/2020/05/14/on-the-cusp-of-adulthood-and-facing-an -uncertain-future-what-we-know-about-gen-z-so-far-2/.

9. "DERANGED TikTok Pronouns!" YouTube video, posted by "Andrew Klavan," October 23, 2021, https://www.youtube.com/watch?v=2AWwxR_rPXo.

10. Anna Brown, "About 5% of Young Adults in the U.S. Say Their Gender Is Different from Their Sex Assigned at Birth," Pew Research Center, June 7, 2022, https://www.pewresearch.org/fact-tank/2022/06/07/about-5-of-young-adults-in-the-u-s-say-their-gender-is-different-from-their-sex-assigned-at-birth/.

11. Abigail Shrier, *Irreversible Damage: The Transgender Craze Seducing Our Daughters* (Washington, DC: Regnery Publishing, 2020).

12. "Preparing for Your Hormone Therapy Visit," Planned Parenthood, accessed April 17, 2023, https://www.plannedparenthood.org/planned-parenthood-western-pennsylvania/patients/introducing-hormone-therapy/preparing-your-hormone-therapy-visit; Loretta Brown, "Handing Out Hormones Like Candy: Planned Parenthood Transitions to Top Hormone Provider for Transgender-Identifying Teens with Little Oversight," *National Catholic Register*, September 9, 2022, https://www.ncregister.com/news/handing-out-hormones-like-candy-planned-parenthood-transitions-to-top-hormone-provider-for-transgender-identifying-teens-with-little-oversight.

13. Jamie Reed, "I Thought I Was Saving Trans Kids," The Free Press, February 9, 2023, https://www.thefp.com/p/i-thought-i-was-saving-trans-kids.

14. "Chooocole," Instagram profile, https://www.instagram.com/chooocole/.

15. Peter Lauria, "Generation Z: Stepping into Financial Independence," Investopedia, August 3, 2022, https://www.investopedia.com/generation-z-stepping-into-financial-independence-5224362.

16. "Bidenflation Adds Up," Senate Republican Policy Committee, July 20, 2022, https://www.rpc.senate.gov/policy-papers/bidenflation-adds-up.

17. "President Biden," Instagram profile, https://www.instagram.com/potus/.

18. "On the Cusp of Adulthood and Facing an Uncertain Future."

19. "Young Americans Still Searching for Real Climate Leadership, According to New ACC Poll," American Conservation Coalition, February 24, 2022, https://www.acc.eco/youth-views-on-climate-and-environment.

20. Alec Tyson, "Gen Z, Millennials Stand Out for Climate Change Activism, Social Media Engagement with Issue," Pew Research Center, May 26, 2021, https://www.pewresearch.org/science/2021/05/26/gen-z-millennials-stand-out-for-climate-change-activism-social-media-engagement-with-issue/.

21. "U.S. Participation in Outdoor Activities by Generation," Statista, https://www.statista.com/statistics/1051784/us-participation-in-outdoor-activities-by-generation/.

22. Kate Eschner, "Lincoln's Signature Laid Groundwork for National Park System," *Smithsonian Magazine*, June 30, 2017, https://www.smithsonianmag.com/smart-news/lincolns-signature-laid-groundwork-national-park-system-180963826/.

23. "Theodore Roosevelt and the National Park System," National Park Service, January 14, 2021, https://www.nps.gov/thrb/learn/historyculture/trand thenpsystem.htm#:~:text=As%20President%20from%201901%20to,of%20 Chickasaw%20National%20Recreation%20Area.

24. "The Origins of EPA," Environmental Protection Agency, June 24, 2022, https://www.epa.gov/history/origins-epa.

25. Cayli Baker, "The Trump Administration's Major Environmental Deregulations," Brookings Institution, December 15, 2020, https://www.brookings .edu/blog/up-front/2020/12/15/the-trump-administrations-major-environmental -deregulations/.

26. "Trump Administration Furthers Commitment to One Trillion Trees Initiative," press release, U.S. Department of the Interior, October 13, 2020, https://www.doi.gov/pressreleases/trump-administration-furthers-commitment -one-trillion-trees-initiative.

27. "President Trump Signs Great American Outdoors Act, Preserving & Protecting National Parks," press release, The White House, August 4, 2020, https://trumpwhitehouse.archives.gov/articles/president-trump-signs -great-american-outdoors-act-preserving-protecting-national-parks/.

28. "On the Cusp of Adulthood and Facing an Uncertain Future."

29. Joshua Rhett Miller, "BLM Removes Website's 'What We Believe' Section That Included Language Blasting Nuclear Family Structure," *New York Post*, September 24, 2020, https://nypost.com/2020/09/24/blm-removes-website -language-blasting-nuclear-family-structure/; Noah Goldberg, "Black Lives Matter Leader Accused of Stealing $10 Million from Organization," *Los Angeles Times*, September 2, 2022, https://www.latimes.com/california/story/2022-09-02 /black-lives-matter-leader-accused-of-stealing-10-million-from-organization; Naomi Schaefer Riley, "The 1619 Project Enters American Classrooms, Adding New Sizzle to Slavery but Significant Cost," Education Next, Fall 2020, https:// www.educationnext.org/1619-project-enters-american-classrooms-adding -new-sizzle-slavery-significant-cost/.

30. Nika Shakhnazarova, "Tax Filings Reveal How BLM Co-Founder Spent Charity Funds," *New York Post*, May 19, 2022, https://nypost.com/2022/05/17/ inside-blm-co-founder-patrisse-cullors-questionable-tax-filings/.

31. Hannah Grossman, "Planned Parenthood Worked on Sex Education Curriculum That Nixed Women, Teen Pregnancy Discussions," Fox News, November 22, 2022, https://www.foxnews.com/media/planned-parenthood-worked -sex-education-curriculum-that-nukes-women-teen-pregnancy-discussions.

32. "Planned Parenthood," Instagram, https://www.instagram.com/p/By StizPJcO6/?hl=en.

33. "Shout Your Abortion," https://shoutyourabortion.com/.

34. "Proximity Review of Planned Parenthood Facilities in Relation to College Campuses," Institute for Pro-Life Advancement, https://www.institutefor prolifeadvancement.org/proximity-review-of-planned-parenthood-facilities -in-relation-to-college-campuses/.

35. Carole Novielli, "50 Million Millennials and Gen Z Dead from Abortion," Live Action, July 21, 2022, https://www.liveaction.org/news/50-million-millenn ial-genz-dead-abortion/.

36. Cassy Fiano-Chesser, "Poll: Millennials and Gen Z Disagree with Biden on Abortion," Live Action, January 20, 2022, https://www.liveaction.org /news/poll-millennials-genz-disagree-biden-abortion/.

37. "Inclusive Language Guide," Colorado State University, October 30, 2018, https://collegian.com/wp-content/uploads/2018/11/Inclusive-Language -Guide_10_30_18.pdf.

38. Emily Ekins, "Poll: 62% of Americans Say They Have Political Views They're Afraid to Share," Cato Institute, July 22, 2020, https://www.cato.org/survey -reports/poll-62-americans-saythey-have-political-views-theyre-afraid-share.

39. Eli Yokley, "Critical Race Theory Is Unpopular Among Young Voters, Polling Shows," Morning Consult, July 8, 2021, https://morningconsult.com/2021 /07/08/gen-z-critical-race-theory-polling/.

40. Ben Sisario, "Morgan Wallen Sets Billboard Chart Record, Again," *New York Times*, September 12, 2022, https://www.nytimes.com/2022/09/12/arts /music/morgan-wallen-dangerous-billboard-chart-record.html.

41. Jason Lipschutz, "Morgan Wallen's 'One Thing at a Time': Five Burning Questions," *Billboard*, March 14, 2023, https://www.billboard.com/music /chart-beat/morgan-wallen-one-thing-at-a-time-five-burning-questions -1235286034/.

42. Olivia Petter, "JK Rowling Faces Backlash after Voicing Support for Researcher Sacked for Transphobic Tweets," The Independent, June 7, 2020, https://web.archive.org/web/20200621051007/https://www.independent.co .uk/life-style/jk-rowling-tweet-women-menstruate-people-transphobia -twitter-a9552866.html.

43. Isabel Brown [@theisabelbrown], TikTok video, February 7, 2023, https://www.tiktok.com/@theisabelbrown/video/7197522552464379182.

44. Samantha Leathers, "JK Rowling Says 'False Claim She Was Cancelled' Drove Up Book Sales: 'Have to Mock Them!'" Express, December 12, 2022, https://www.express.co.uk/celebrity-news/1708576/jk-rowling-cancelled -trans-twitter-row-harry-potter-net-worth-books-news.

45. Matthew Byrd, "Hogwarts Legacy's Sales Numbers Set Records for Warner Bros. Games," Den of Geek, February 23, 2023, https://www.denofgeek .com/games/hogwarts-legacys-sales-numbers-records-revenue/.

46. Ryan Smith, "Failed Harry Potter Boycott Has Actually Boosted JK Rowling's Fortune," *Newsweek*, February 3, 2023, https://www.newsweek.com /hogwarts-legacy-boycott-failed-jk-rowling-harry-potter-1778891.

47. Dana Hall, "JK Rowling Turned Down by 12 Publishers before Finding Success with Harry Potter Books," Rise Up Eight, https://riseupeight.org /jk-rowling-harry-potter-books/.

48. "What We Have Done," SEE International, https://www.seeintl.org /what-we-have-done/.

49. Charlotte Benton, "MrBeast: Why Has YouTuber Faced Criticism for Blind Surgery Video?" BBC News, February 1, 2023, https://www.bbc.com/news /newsbeat-64490431.

50. Zatzman [@TheZatzman], tweet, January 29, 2023, https://twitter.com /TheZatzman/status/1619728882755850240.

51. Carissa Cheong, "YouTuber MrBeast Defends Himself after a Video in Which He Said He Was 'Curing' 1,000 Blind People Divided Viewers," Insider, January 31, 2023, https://www.insider.com/mrbeast-criticism-blindness -video-response-2023-1.

52. LolOverruled [@LolOverruled], tweet, January 28, 2023, https://twitter .com/LolOverruled/status/1619538554555895808.

53. MrBeast [@MrBeast], tweet, January 30, 2023, https://twitter.com /MrBeast/status/1620195967008907264?ref_src=twsrc%5Etfw%7Ctw camp%5Etweetembed%7Ctwterm%5E1620195967008907264%7Ctwgr%5 E14008b694d77461778152fad31b96214b11206f9%7Ctwcon%5Es1_&ref_url=https %3A%2F%2Fwww.insider.com%2Fmrbeast-criticism-blindness-video -response-2023-1.

54. Cheong, "YouTuber MrBeast Defends Himself after a Video in Which He Said He Was 'Curing' 1,000 Blind People Divided Viewers."

55. "MrBeast Philanthropy," YouTube. https://www.youtube.com/@Beast Philanthropy.

Chapter 5

1. Lee Drutman, "America Is Now the Divided Republic the Framers Feared," *The Atlantic*, January 2, 2020, https://www.theatlantic.com/ideas /archive/2020/01/two-party-system-broke-constitution/604213/.

2.   Anna Brown, "Most Democrats Who Are Looking for a Relationship Would Not Consider Dating a Trump Voter," Pew Research Center, April 24, 2020, https://www.pewresearch.org/fact-tank/2020/04/24/most-democrats-who -are-looking-for-a-relationship-would-not-consider-dating-a-trump-voter/.

3.   Tovia Smith, "'Dude, I'm Done': When Politics Tears Families and Friendships Apart," NPR, October 27, 2020, https://www.npr.org/2020/10/27 /928209548/dude-i-m-done-when-politics-tears-families-and-friendships-apart.

4.   "As Partisan Hostility Grows, Signs of Frustration with the Two-Party System," Pew Research Center, August 9, 2022, https://www.pewresearch.org /politics/2022/08/09/as-partisan-hostility-grows-signs-of-frustration-with -the-two-party-system/.

5.   "The Vanderbilt Unity Index," Vanderbilt Project on Unity and American Democracy, Vanderbilt University, https://www.vanderbilt.edu/unity/vanderbilt -unity-index/.

6.   Rikki Schlott, "Gen Z Is Done with Our Two-Party System and Will Force Change," *New York Post*, November 13, 2021, https://nypost.com/2021/11/13/gen -z-is-done-with-our-two-party-system-and-will-force-change/.

7.   Julia Johnson, "More than Half Millennials, Generation Z Independents: Poll," *Washington Examiner*, August 20, 2022, https://www.washingtonexam iner.com/news/more-than-half-millennials-generation-z-independents-poll.

8.   "As Partisan Hostility Grows, Signs of Frustration with the Two-Party System."

9.   Brad Bannon, "Gen Z Ready to Make Its Mark on Congress," The Hill, August 30, 2022, https://thehill.com/opinion/campaign/3668125-gen -z-ready-to-make-its-mark-on-congress/.

10.   Elena Moore, "Maxwell Frost, First Gen Z Candidate, Wins Primary," NPR, August 23, 2022, https://www.npr.org/sections/2022-live-primary-election-race-results /2022/08/23/1119003972/maxwell-frost-first-gen-z-candidate-wins-primary.

11.   Umar Farooq, "How Florida Progressive Maxwell Frost Abandoned Palestine," Middle East Eye, August 29, 2022, https://www.middleeasteye.net /news/how-florida-progressive-maxwell-frost-abandoned-palestine.

12.   Svante Myrick, "The Gen Z Politics That Will Make or Break America," *Chicago Sun-Times*, January 17, 2023, https://chicago.suntimes.com /2023/1/17/ 23559244/gen-z-politics-congress-health-care-climate-change-economics -svante-myrick-column.

13.   Bridget Bowman, "GOP Leadership Split in New Hampshire House Primary," *Meet the Press*, NBC News, September 9, 2022, https://www .nbcnews.com/meet-the-press/meetthepressblog/gop-leadership-split-new -hampshire-house-primary-rcna47009.

14. Jessica Bryant, "COVID-19, College and Gen Z: What the Pandemic Has Taught Us," BestColleges, July 6, 2022, https://www.bestcolleges.com /news/analysis/2021/11/22/gen-z-college-survey-covid-pandemic/.

15. Juliana Stancampiano, "Why Gen Z Cares Less about Getting a 4-Year College Degree," Fast Company, May 31, 2022, https://www.fastcompany.com /90755962/why-gen-z-cares-less-about-getting-a-4-year-college-degree.

16. Elissa Nadworny, "Skilled Trade Programs Are Booming After College Enrollment Dropped in the Pandemic," NPR, March 20, 2022, https://www .npr.org/2022/03/20/1087766188/skilledtrade-programs-are-booming-after -college-enrollment-dropped-in-the-pande.

17. Aastha Singhal, "Gen Z Learners Are Taking Up DIY Education," *Entrepreneur*, September 18, 2019, https://www.entrepreneur.com/en-in/news-and -trends/gen-z-learners-are-taking-up-diy-education/339636; Christopher Rim, "The Problem Facing Liberal Arts Education Is Not Subject Matter, It's Application," *Forbes*, January 11, 2023, https://www.forbes.com/sites/christopherrim /2023/01/11/the-problem-facing-liberal-arts-education-is-not-subject-matter -its-application/#:~:text=On%20one%20hand%2C%20liberal%20arts,had %20persisted%20for%20years%20prior.

18. Hans Johnson, "More Students Are Earning STEM Degrees," Public Policy Institute of California, July 31, 2018, https://www.ppic.org/blog/ more-students-are-earning-stem-degrees/.

19. Siel Ju, "35 CEOs Who Never Finished College," Stacker, October 18, 2019, https://stacker.com/education/35-ceos-who-never-finished-college; Abe Selig, "Generation Influence: Reaching Gen Z in the New Digital Paradigm," WP Engine, December 9, 2022, https://wpengine.com/resources/gen-z-2020.

20. Shafin Tejani, "Gen Z Entrepreneurs," *Worth*, April 16, 2021, https://www .worth.com/gen-z-entrepreneurs/#:~:text=Gen%20Z%20is%20rapidly%20 becoming,to%20start—their%20own%20business.&text=But%20they%20 also%20bring%20some,generation%20an%20edge%20in%20business.

21. Aashna Shah, "Microsoft Finds Gen Z Is Redefining the Idea of Work Hustle," CNBC, June 18, 2022, https://www.cnbc.com/2022/06/18/microsoft- finds-gen-z-is-redefining-the-idea-of-work-hustle.html.

22. John Koetsier, "2 Million Creators Make 6-Figure Incomes on You-Tube, Instagram, Twitch Globally," *Forbes*, October 5, 2020, https://www .forbes.com/sites/johnkoetsier/2020/10/05/2-million-creators-make-6-figure -incomes-on-youtube-instagram-twitch-globally/?sh=1f086c0323be.

23. Orianna Rose Royle, "Gen Z Polyworking: One Job Not Pay Enough? Flexibility? Paychex," *Fortune*, March 20, 2023, https://fortune.com/2023/03/20/gen -z-polyworking-one-job-not-pay-enough-flexibility-paychex/.

24. Shah, "Microsoft Finds Gen Z Is Redefining the Idea of Work Hustle."

25. Lindsay Ellis, "Your Gen Z Co-Worker Is Hustling More Than You Think," *Wall Street Journal*, April 11, 2023, https://www.wsj.com/articles/your-gen-z-co-worker-is-hustling-more-than-you-think-7717bc5e.

26. "44% of Americans Have a Side Hustle Amid Inflation, Most Popular With Gen Z'ers," PR Newswire, December 7, 2022, https://www.prnewswire.com/news-releases/44-of-americans-have-a-side-hustle-amid-inflation-most-popular-with-gen-zers-301697437.html.

27. David Bauder, "Trust in Media Low, Misinform, Mislead, Biased: Republicans, Democrats—Poll—Gallup," *Fortune*, February 15, 2023, https://fortune.com/2023/02/15/trust-in-media-low-misinform-mislead-biased-republicans-democrats-poll-gallup/.

28. Mark Joyella, "CNN Hits 10-Year Low in Prime Time as Fox News Glides to Victory in February Cable News Ratings," *Forbes*, February 28, 2023, https://www.forbes.com/sites/markjoyella/2023/02/28/cnn-hits-10-year-low-in-prime-time-as-fox-news-glides-to-victory-in-february-cable-news-ratings/?sh=1a75e1d77d09.

29. "Leading Cable News Networks in the United States in February 2023, by Number of Primetime Viewers," Statista, https://www.statista.com/statistics/373814/cable-news-network-viewership-usa/#:~:text=In%20February%202023%2C%20Fox%20News,MSNBC%20had%20just%20119%20thousand.

30. "TikTok Hits 150 Million US Monthly Users, Up from 100 Million in 2020," Business of Fashion, March 21, 2023, Reuters, https://www.businessoffashion.com/news/technology/tiktok-hits-150-million-us-monthly-users-up-from-100-million-in-2020/#:~:text=TikTok%20said%20on%20Monday%20the,House%20Energy%20and%20Commerce%20Committee; Mansoor Iqbal, "TikTok Statistics," Business of Apps, January 9, 2023, https://www.businessofapps.com/data/tik-tok-statistics/.

31. Katarina Eva Matsa, "More Americans Are Getting News on TikTok, Bucking the Trend on Other Social Media Sites," Pew Research Center, October 21, 2022, https://www.pewresearch.org/fact-tank/2022/10/21/more-americans-are-getting-news-on-tiktok-bucking-the-trend-on-other-social-media-sites/.

32. Representative Jeff Jackson, "@jeffjacksonnc," TikTok, https://www.tiktok.com/@jeffjacksonnc?lang=en.

33. Libs of Tik Tok, "@libsoftiktok," Twitter, https://twitter.com/libsoftiktok.

34. Morgan Sung, "Twitch Streamers Want Political Pundits of Their Own: Generation Hasanabi, Frogan," NBC News, November 8, 2022, https://www.nbcnews.com/tech/twitch-streamers-want-political-pundits-generation-hasanabi-frogan-rcna56094.

35. Blaine Polhamus, "Who Is Hasan Piker, Prolific Twitch Political Streamer, Explained," Dot Esports, July 7, 2022, https://dotesports.com/streaming/news /who-is-hasan-piker-prolific-twitch-political-streamer-explained.

36. "HasanAbi Videos," Twitch, https://www.twitch.tv/hasanabi/videos.

37. "The Comments Section," YouTube, https://www.youtube.com/@The CommentsSection.

38. "Amala Ekpunobi: Unapologetic," YouTube, https://www.youtube .com/@AmalaEkpunobiUnapologetic.

39. Rumble, last modified September 18, 2022, https://corp.rumble.com/.

40. Steven Crowder, "@scrowder," Twitter, March 20, 2023, https://twitter .com/scrowder/status/1637825472758259712.

41. "Generation Z Characteristics: What Businesses Should Know About the Next Wave of Consumers," NCR Blog, November 10, 2020, https://www .ncr.com/blogs/generation-z-characteristics-what-businesses-should-know-about-the-next-wave-of-consumers.

42 Ulta Beauty, "The Beauty of... Girlhood with Dylan Mulvaney," You-Tube, October 13, 2022, https://www.youtube.com/watch?v=h1Z_xPQctgE.

43. Abby Monteil, Samantha Riedel, and James Factora, "The Dylan Mulvaney and Bud Light Fiasco: Everything You Need to Know," *Them*, July 12, 2023, https://www.them.us/story/dylan-mulvaney-bud-light-drama-explained.

44. Chantelle Marcelle, "Duolingo Growth Marketing Case Study," Chantelle Marcelle.com, https://chantellemarcelle.com/duolingo-growth-marketing-case -study/#:~:text=Duolingo%20became%20a%20growth%20marketing, felt%20 authentic%2C%20not%20horribly%20forced.

45. "Zaria Parvez," *Forbes*, https://www.forbes.com/profile/zaria-parvez /?sh=1e99704a6127.

46. "Gen Z Purpose Study," Cone Communications, https://conecomm .com/cone-gen-z-purpose-study/.

47. "Accenture Retail Customer Journey Research 2017 Infographic," Accenture, 2017, https://www.accenture.com/_acnmedia/PDF-44/Accenture-Retail -Customer-Journey-Research-2017-Infographic.pdf#zoom=50.

Chapter 6

1. Taylor Lorenz, "Facebook, TikTok Targeted in Victory for Democrats' Antitrust Push," *Washington Post*, March 30, 2022, https://www.washingtonpost .com/technology/2022/03/30/facebook-tiktok-targeted-victory/.

2.   Cristiano Lima, "What Are the Facebook Papers?" *Washington Post*, October 26, 2021, https://www.washingtonpost.com/technology/2021/10/25/what-are-the-facebook-papers/.

3.   Carol Lee, "TikTok Now Has 150 Million Active Users in US, CEO Tells Congress," NBC News, March 19, 2023, https://www.nbcnews.com/politics/congress/tiktok-now-150-million-active-users-us-ceo-tell-congress-rcna75607; "What the Rise of TikTok Says About Generation Z," Forbes Tech Council, *Forbes*, July 7, 2020, https://www.forbes.com/sites/forbestechcouncil/2020/07/07/what-the-rise-of-tiktok-says-about-generation-z/?sh=e16e3d865490.

4.   "Gbp97 on TikTok," March 23, 2023, https://www.tiktok.com/@gbp97/video/7213775012883434795?_t=8bZSLNKOIo3&_r=1.

5.   "Motherboardvice on TikTok," March 23, 2023, https://www.tiktok.com/@motherboardvice/video/7213780130202750250?_r=1&_t=8bZS-J99SW5e.

6.   "Nowthispolitics on TikTok," March 23, 2023, https://www.tiktok.com/@nowthispolitics/video/7213856534080605483?_r=1&_t=8bZSQFNqRkk.

7.   "Rubin_Allergy on TikTok," March 23, 2023, https://www.tiktok.com/@rubin_allergy/video/7213800333162630446?_r=1&_t=8bZSNUCb1tz.

8.   "Kes.io on TikTok," March 23, 2023, https://www.tiktok.com/@kes.io/video/7214994392707321134?_r=1&_t=8bZSXV2ouUQ.

9.   "Rep. Dan Crenshaw's $META Investment Jumps 51% Amidst Possible TikTok Ban," Capitol Trades, March 27, 2023, https://www.capitoltrades.com/buzz/282546088#.

10.   Ronald Reagan, "Inaugural Address (Public Ceremony)," East Portico of the United States Capitol Building, January 5, 1967, Reagan Library, https://www.reaganlibrary.gov/archives/speech/january-5-1967-inaugural-address-public-ceremony.

11.   "Lincoln's House Divided Speech," Lincoln Home National Historic Site, National Park Service, last modified January 4, 2022, https://www.nps.gov/liho/learn/historyculture/housedivided.htm.

12.   Katie Rogers, "White House Hosts Social Media Summit and Facebook and Twitter Aren't Invited," *New York Times*, July 11, 2019, https://www.nytimes.com/2019/07/11/us/politics/white-house-social-media-summit.html.

13.   Alison Durkee, "Trump's Social Media Summit Was a Far-Right Troll Convention," *Vanity Fair*, July 8, 2019, https://www.vanityfair.com/news/2019/07/trump-social-media-summit-far-right; Peter Kafka, "The White House's Social Media Summit Was a Circus Full of Conspiracy Theories,"

Vox, July 11, 2019, https://www.vox.com/recode/2019/7/11/20690744white-house-social-media-summit-trump-conspiracy-twitter-facebook-youtube.

14. "Number of Twitter Users in the US," Oberlo, https://www.oberlo.com/statistics/number-of-twitter-users-in-the-us; TikTok Newsroom, "150 Million U.S. Users," March 21, 2023, https://newsroom.tiktok.com/en-us/150-m-us-users.

15. Sophia Cai, "Biden's Digital Strategy: An Army of Influencers," Axios, April 9, 2023, https://www.axios.com/2023/04/09/bidens-digital-strategy-an-army-of-influencers.

Chapter 7

1. Kathryn Robinson, "Survey: Most Kids Spend More than 5 Hours a Day on Social Media or Video Games," WKRC, November 28, 2022, https://local12.com/news/local/survey-most-kids-spend-more-than-5-hours-a-day-on-social-media-or-video-games.

2. Emily Shapiro, "Parkland School Shooting 5 Years Later: Remembering the 17 Victims," ABC News, February 14, 2023, https://abcnews.go.com/US/teacher-coach14-year-freshman-florida-high-school-massacre/story?id=53092879.

3. March for Our Lives, "Mission Story," retrieved April 17, 2023, from https://marchforourlives.com/mission-story/.

4. Ryan Gaydos, "Riley Gaines Details Harrowing Situation at SFSU: 'I Feared for My Life in That Moment,'" Fox News, April 12, 2023, https://www.foxnews.com/sports/riley-gaines-details-harrowing-situation-sfsu-feared-my-life-moment.

5. Amy Larson, "SFSU President Says Riley Gaines Event Was 'Deeply Traumatic' for Trans Community," KRON4, April 11, 2023, https://www.kron4.com/news/bay-area/sfsu-president-says-riley-gaines-event-was-deeply-traumatic-for-trans-community/#:~:text=SFSU%20president%20says%20Riley%20Gaines,deeply%20traumatic%27%20for%20trans%20community&text=SAN%20FRANCISCO%20(KRON)%20%E2%80%94%20San,who%20claims%20she%20was%20assaulted.

6. Johanna Alonso, "Shouting Down Speakers Who Offend," Inside Higher Ed, April 13, 2023, www.insidehighered.com/news/students/free-speech/2023/04/13/shouting-down-speakers-who-offend.

7. Gianna Melillo, "Here Are the Oldest US Presidents to Ever Hold Office," The Hill, November 21, 2022, https://thehill.com/changing-america/enrichment/arts-culture/3744771-here-are-the-oldest-us-presidents-to-ever-hold-office/.

8.   "Charles Schumer," Congress.gov, https://www.congress.gov/member /charles-schumer/S000148.

9.   "Mitch McConnell," Congress.gov, https://www.congress.gov/member /mitch-mcconnell/M000355.

10. "Nancy Pelosi," Congress.gov, https://www.congress.gov/member /nancy-pelosi/P000197.

11. "Why?" Run GenZ, https://rungenz.com/why/.

12. "Rising Stars," Run GenZ, https://rungenz.com/rising-stars/.

Chapter 8

1.   Jarett Stepman, "Pride in America Has Collapsed for Gen Z. Here's What We Should Do," The Daily Signal, January 13, 2023, https://www.dailysignal .com/2023/01/13/why-only-16-of-gen-z-are-proud-to-be-an-american-and-what -we-should-do-about-it/.

2.   John 15:18-19, The Bible, New International Version, www.biblegateway .com/passage/?search=John%2015%3A18-25&version=NIV.

about the author

Isabel Brown is a full-time independent content creator and livestreamer, giving a voice to Generation Z, breaking down culture's most important topics to thousands of viewers in a real-time, authentic format. Working as an independent creator, Isabel's streams and other content across social media platforms reach millions of people around the world daily. She is also the host of two independently produced series, *Outdated*, breaking down the lies of modern dating culture and replacing them with the truth, and *Domus*, discussing faith and the Church through a Gen Z lens.

She self-published her first bestselling book, *Frontlines: Finding My Voice on an American College Campus*, in February 2021, and is so excited to continue amplifying the cultural impact of Generation Z through *The End of the Alphabet*.

As a voice for her generation, Isabel regularly appears on national television and radio programming, domestically on Fox News, Newsmax, One America News, Newsy, & BoldTV, and internationally on Sky News UK, Sky News Arabia, BBC Radio, and French and German Public Broadcasting. You might also recognize her from her photo on the cover of *Newsweek* magazine.

She frequently creates content for organizations making cultural change in America and around the world, including Turning Point USA, Students for Life, the Daily Wire, The Conversationalist, Evie Magazine, PragerU, LiveAction, and more. Before becoming a full-time creator and working in media, Isabel earned her bachelor's degree in Biomedical Sciences from Colorado State University and her master's degree in Biomedical Sciences Policy and Advocacy from Georgetown University. In college, she worked for both the United States Senate and the White House under the Trump administration.

Today, Isabel lives in Miami and loves embracing adventure in the sunshine state with her fiancé, Brock, and her corgi, Liberty!